BEYOND THE RUN

BEYOND THE RUN

The Emanuel Harmon Farm
at Gettysburg

Andrew I. Dalton

Design and production by Bare Hands Design, Gettysburg, Pennsylvania
Printed and bound in the United States of America

ISBN: 978-1-5193028-7-8 (paper)

Cover photo courtesy of William A. Frassanito

To my grandfather, William Iannello

Contents

Part 2

1865–1947: The Katalysine Spring

1947–2011: Epilogue

Foreword

In the aftermath of the Battle of Gettysburg vast numbers of people were attracted to the fields in which the great battle had been fought. This popularity only increased following the dedication of the Soldier's National Cemetery and the development of the Gettysburg Battlefield Memorial Association. Very quickly, enterprising townspeople became aware of the opportunity presented by this sudden interest in Gettysburg. Hotels and taverns expanded their businesses and enjoyed great prosperity. There was an increase in the number of stables, as carriages driven by local guides conducted parties all over the battlefield. In addition, relics and souvenirs of the fight were sold all over the town. While many provided services that were much needed and greatly desired, others were simply taking advantage of the situation in an effort to make a quick buck.

One of the most ambitious projects undertaken in the years immediately following the battle was the bottling and distribution of water from a spring west of Gettysburg on the farm of Emanuel Harmon. Did the water of the spring actually have the medicinal qualities and great benefit to the public as claimed? Or was it just an elaborate scheme created by Harmon, in an effort to recover the losses suffered when his farm was destroyed by Confederate forces on the afternoon of July 1, 1863? The truth of the matter may never be known for sure, but perhaps it was a little of both. In 1869 the popularity of the spring led to the construction of a large hotel. Shortly after its opening, the Gettysburg Springs Hotel was the site of the first major gathering of veterans to the battlefield, and continued to host such events over the next few decades.

Since the early days of the Gettysburg battlefield there has been a struggle between the forces of memorialization and commercialization. And the story of the Springs Hotel epitomizes that conflict. On the one hand, heavy visitation brought attention to the site, and highlighted its important role in the battle. On the other hand, the fact that the site was privately owned by a group of wealthy investors prohibited its purchase by those seeking its preservation. And while other areas of the field were being protected for future generations, this site was transferred from developer to developer, its role in the battle ignored and largely forgotten. Only recently, has a portion of the original Harmon Farm been purchased and turned over to the Gettysburg National Military Park, ensuring that the ground on both sides of Willoughby's Run can now be restored to its 1863 appearance. The result of this will be a more complete interpretation of the fighting in and around Herbst Woods on the morning and afternoon of July 1 from the perspective of not only the Union defenders, but that of the Confederate attackers as well.

In this micro-history of the Harmon Farm, Andrew Dalton has provided us with the first extensive published narrative of this important site. He covers not only the battle, but the early history of the site and its development as one of the premier Gettysburg commercial attractions. He has spent considerable time and effort in gathering sources from a variety of repositories, providing us with a well written and well balanced treatment of this fascinating story.

Timothy H. Smith

Gettysburg, Pennsylvania

May 2013

Preface

My family moved to Gettysburg when I was four, and I soon became fascinated with the battlefield and town; many years later, I still am.

Over the past 150 years, much has been written about the Battle of Gettysburg. And yet there are always stories waiting to be told. Some historic properties, like the Emanuel Harmon farm, have received little attention. Given its proximity to Gettysburg, it is surprising that little research has been done concerning this land.

I've lived near the Emanuel Harmon farm for most of my life. Over the years I have spent countless hours roaming its fields on foot, on a bicycle, and even on cross-country skis. As I matured, my interest in the property grew and developed, nurtured by some of Gettysburg's finest historians.

This project began as a quest to research the role that my neighborhood played as a staging area for Confederate attacks during the first day of the Battle of Gettysburg. I soon discovered stories more intriguing than I'd ever imagined. Better yet, much of the information had never been made available to the public. The catalyst of this project was the story of 16-year-old Amelia E. Harmon, who witnessed the battle from a farmhouse along Old Mill Road. She later wrote an account of the fighting that occurred near her home. Accurate in nearly every detail, her words inspired me to dig deeper into the history of the property.

Several manuscripts have been particularly helpful to me during my research: "The Significance of the Harmon Farm and the Springs Hotel Woods" by Kathleen Georg Harrison, "The Gettysburg Springs Hotel" by Donald R. Heiges, and "The Burning of the Home of General 'Stonewall' Jackson's Uncle by the Rebels during the First Day's Battle of Gettysburg, July 1, 1863" by Colonel Jacob M. Sheads. These historians sparked my interest through their writings, and their research is invaluable for anyone studying the Harmon farm.

Photographic Abbreviations

121RPV	History of the 121st Regiment Pennsylvania Volunteers, an Account from the Ranks by the Survivors' Association, 1906
ACHS	Adams County Historical Society
AIDC	Andrew I. Dalton Collection
CVM	*Confederate Veteran Magazine*
ENHS	Eisenhower National Historic Site
GNMP	Gettysburg National Military Park
HSRBNC	Histories of the Several Regiments and Battalions from North Carolina by Walter Clark, 1901
IMA	Indianapolis Museum of Art
LOC	Library of Congress
LODNC	Lives of Distinguished North Carolinians with Illustrations and Speeches, 1898
PGS	Pennsylvania Geological Survey
PHOTCW	The Photographic History of the Civil War, 1912
SBC	Sue Boardman Collection
SCMLGC	Courtesy of Special Collections, Musselman Library, Gettysburg College
SROC	Seward R. Osborne Collection
USAMHI	United States Army Military History Institute
USPTO	United States Patent and Trademark Office
VMI	Courtesy of the Virginia Military Institute Archives
FRASSANITO COLL.	William A. Frassanito Collection

Acknowledgments

Many people have advised me in the process of researching and writing this book. First and foremost I thank historian and Licensed Battlefield Guide Timothy H. Smith, whose remarkable knowledge of both the town and the Battle of Gettysburg guided my research. He has been an invaluable mentor, and I look forward to learning more from him in the future.

The staff of the Adams County Historical Society have been especially welcoming and helpful. I am indebted to Larry Bolin, who graciously worked to improve my manuscript. I also thank Rodger and Vickie Rex for their support and encouragement.

I am honored that renowned historian and former Adams County Historical Society Director, the late Dr. Charles H. Glatfelter, found time to help me with my research. I thank him gratefully and am honored to have known him.

Also, I thank Gerry and Arlene O'Brien, who have supported my interest in history for as long as I can remember.

Many other notable Gettysburg historians and authors have helped me in one way or another. Among them is William A. Frassanito, whose remarkable knowledge of early Gettysburg photography was a tremendous asset to this project. Others include: Wayne Motts, Scott Hartwig, John Heiser, Matt Atkinson, Barb Sanders, and Ben Neely. Thank you all.

Finally, I thank my grandfather, William Iannello, and my parents, Terence Dalton and Kathleen Iannello. They have been unfailing in their support and encouragement throughout the process of researching and writing this book. Thank you for your attention to my endless lectures and for your good-natured participation in the many Gettysburg "quizzes" to which I subjected you.

Introduction

West of Gettysburg, a creek known locally as Willoughby's Run meanders through the quiet fields and pastures that are characteristic of southern Pennsylvania. On July 1, 1863, its banks were lined with the corpses of soldiers who died during the first day of the Battle of Gettysburg. When the smoke cleared that evening, the area west of the creek was a smoldering ruin. Of one of the finest residences in the area—the Harmon farmhouse—only charred brick and ashes remained.

At that time no one knew that Willoughby's Run would become a "boundary" for those who studied and wrote about the battle. Few early visitors ventured across the stream to the fields beyond, and the area's bloody history was quickly overshadowed by the 1865 discovery of a "healing spring" nearby. The spring became so popular that in 1869 a hotel was constructed near the site to accommodate the many visitors who came to sample its waters.

Nevertheless, the Harmon farm and its medicinal spring were largely forgotten, despite its historical importance and the popularity of its waters.

◆

The tract of land which became the Harmon farm lies in Cumberland Township between the Chambersburg Pike and the Fairfield Road. Willoughby's Run, which flows today as it did 150 years ago, forms its eastern boundary; the eastern slope of Herr's Ridge, its western boundary. The Mill Road, today called Old Mill Road, runs directly through the property and once led to a saw and grist mill on Marsh Creek.[1] In 1851 the tract was subdivided, and the land north of the Mill Road became the Emanuel Harmon farm. After the Battle of Gettysburg, Harmon purchased the land south of this road and restored the farm to its original acreage.

Most of the 1863 Harmon farm has been preserved and is now owned by the National Park Service. The woods owned in part by Emanuel Harmon, later known as the Springs Hotel Woods, are also now part of the Gettysburg National Military Park.

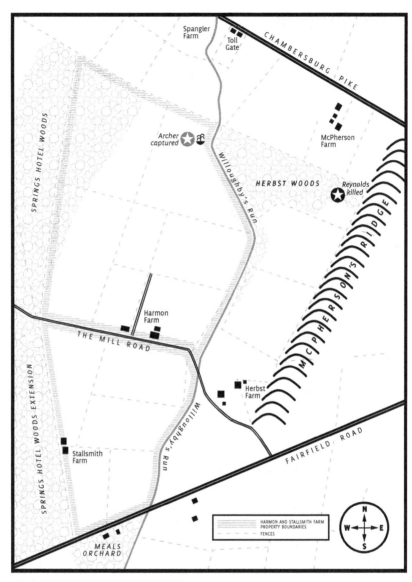

Spangler
Farm

Toll
Gate

CHAMBERSBURG PIKE

SPRINGS HOTEL WOODS

Archer
captured

McPherson
Farm

Willoughby's Run

HERBST WOODS

Reynolds
killed

McPHERSON'S RIDGE

Harmon
Farm

THE MILL ROAD

SPRINGS HOTEL WOODS EXTENSION

Herbst
Farm

Stallsmith
Farm

Willoughby's Run

FAIRFIELD ROAD

HARMON AND STALLSMITH FARM
PROPERTY BOUNDARIES

FENCES

N
W   E
S

MEALS
ORCHARD

AN 1863 DEPICTION OF THE HARMON FARM

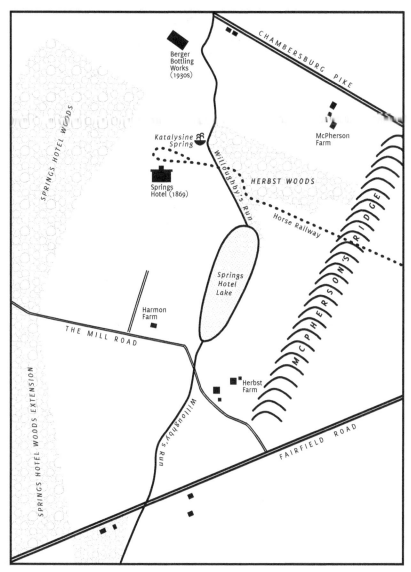

CHAMBERSBURG PIKE

Berger
Bottling
Works
(1930s)

McPherson
Farm

Katalysine Spring

Willoughby's Run

HERBST WOODS

SPRINGS HOTEL WOODS

Springs
Hotel (1869)

Horse Railway

M C P H E R S O N ' S   R I D G E

Springs
Hotel
Lake

Harmon
Farm

THE MILL ROAD

SPRINGS HOTEL WOODS EXTENSION

Herbst
Farm

Willoughby's Run

FAIRFIELD ROAD

A POST-CIVIL WAR MAP SHOWING IMPROVEMENTS ASSOCIATED WITH THE KATALYSINE SPRING

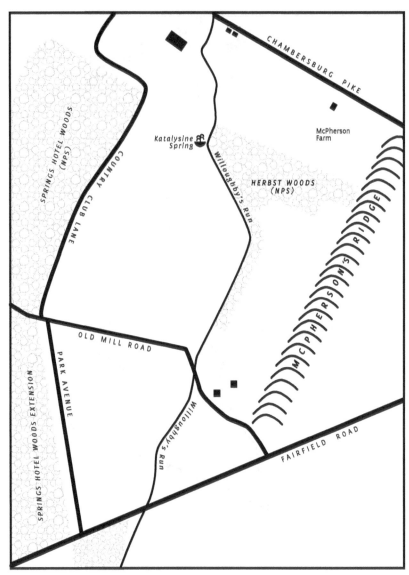

CHAMBERSBURG PIKE

SPRINGS HOTEL WOODS (NPS)

COUNTRY CLUB LANE

Katalysine Spring

McPherson Farm

HERBST WOODS (NPS)

Willoughby's Run

McPHERSON'S RIDGE

OLD MILL ROAD

SPRINGS HOTEL WOODS EXTENSION

PARK AVENUE

Willoughby's Run

FAIRFIELD ROAD

A MODERN DEPICTION OF THE HARMON FARM SHOWING CURRENT ROADS

Part 1

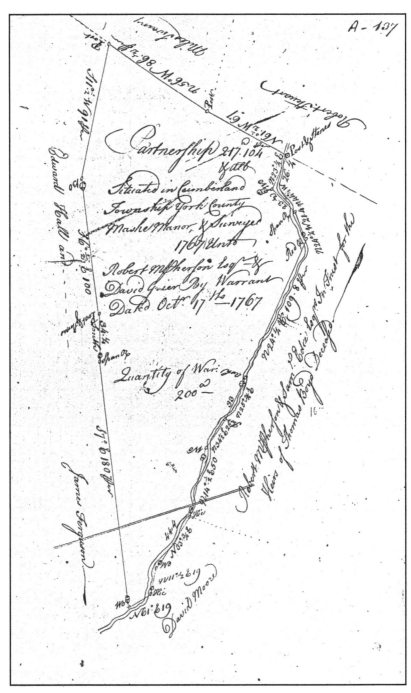

AN EARLY SURVEY OF THE PROPERTY (ACHS)

1798–1863: Quiet Farm Field

Early Ownership

On January 25, 1798, William Penn's heirs sold the property that became the Harmon farm to William McPherson, a prominent Gettysburg citizen. According to the 1798 Direct Tax, two structures were located on the farm at that time: a log dwelling house and an old log stable.[2]

When duty called, McPherson fought in the Revolutionary War and was captured during the Battle of Long Island. After his release from nearly two years' imprisonment, he returned to Gettysburg, entered politics, and became a key advocate for the creation of Adams County in 1800. Father of seven, William McPherson died in 1832 at age 75. He is buried in Evergreen Cemetery in the family plot.[3]

In 1814 McPherson sold the farm to Frederick Keefer. Like McPherson, Keefer probably never lived on the property. At that time he was tavern keeper of what is now the Gettysburg Hotel and ran a cabinet shop at the east end of York Street. In 1819 Keefer sold the farm to Rev. Charles G. McLean, a Presbyterian minister. Keefer died on November 6, 1834.[4]

Charles G. McLean

Charles G. McLean was born in Ireland in 1787. His father, John McLean, was a surgeon in the British navy and apparently died at sea during an expedition to Africa. His widow later married the Rev. James Gray and, with Charles, the couple moved across the Atlantic to Philadelphia. Subsequently Charles attended the University of Pennsylvania and became a Presbyterian clergyman.

In 1815 Charles McLean married Helen Miller, described as "the handsomest" of the Miller girls. Helen was also the aunt of Eleanor Junkin, first wife of Confederate Gen. Thomas "Stonewall" Jackson. It seems plausible that Eleanor might have visited her aunt and uncle at their farm west of Gettysburg during the 1820s and '30s. Helen's brother-in-law, George Junkin, also a clergyman, was president of Washington College in Lexington, Virginia, and later became the first president of Lafayette College in Easton, Pennsylvania.[5]

The McLeans purchased the Harmon farm in 1819. Around that time Charles began to serve as minister of two Presbyterian congregations in the area.[6]

After moving to the farm, the McLeans started a family and began to make significant improvements to the property. However, tragedy struck in October 1819 when their son died in infancy; Helen McLean died just three years later.

Despite these losses, Charles pressed forward with property improvements, finally advertising the "valuable farm, on which he resides" for sale in 1841. His 224 acres of land were "well adapted for grain and grass" and "under good fence." The property included a newly-constructed two-story "double brick house" with four rooms on the first floor and five on the second.[7] At some point a cupola had been added to the roof, although this feature was not mentioned in the advertisement.

REV. CHARLES G. MCLEAN (IMA)

The structure faced south on the crest of a small ridge just north of the Mill Road and just west of Willoughby's Run. Because it dominated the surrounding countryside, the location was often described as "a commanding position." Behind the Harmon house was a "two story brick wash and smoke house with a never failing pump and cistern, with all the usual outbuildings." Just west of the main house stood a large "double stone bank barn," a wagon shed, and a corn crib. The "large log tenant house" remained on the property, probably along what later became the Springs Hotel Woods near the Fairfield Road. Between these structures and Willoughby's Run was a large orchard containing apple, peach, cherry, and plum trees.[8]

In 1849 Rev. McLean sold the property to John Miller. McLean moved on to serve congregations in Baltimore, Maryland, and Fort Plains, New York, then later founded a female seminary in Indianapolis, Indiana. He died in Indianapolis in 1860 at age 73 from "congestion of the brain." His body was later returned to Gettysburg and interred in Evergreen Cemetery beside members of his family.[9]

Property Subdivision

John Miller, owner of the farm from 1849 to 1851, actually lived on the property. He is listed on the 1850 census as a 45-year-old farmer with a considerable real estate value. Miller and his family, all New Yorkers, were sharing the large house with Joseph Eaton and his family, also from New York.[10]

On October 28, 1850, Miller subdivided his property and sold everything south of the Mill Road to Peter Stallsmith. However, this property was probably never occupied by the Stallsmith family; post-battle maps indicate that William Keefauver lived on the land in a wooden house along what is now Park Avenue.[11] Peter Stallsmith died in 1862, but his heirs did not sell the property until after the Battle of Gettysburg.

In 1851 John Miller sold part of the Springs Hotel Woods to the directors of the Adams County Alms House. In October of that year he sold the remaining acres north of the Mill Road to Samuel Herbst, a town councilman and member of the Gettysburg Fire Company.[12] It is unlikely that Herbst ever resided on the property as records confirm that he lived elsewhere during this period.

In 1857 Herbst sold his land to James Cooper for $5,000. Cooper, a U.S. Congressman who would serve as a brigadier general during the Civil War, owned the property for just six months. Although he sold the land to Emanuel Harmon in October 1857, Cooper's name appears above the farm on the 1858 Adams County map.[13]

At the time of the Battle of Gettysburg in 1863, Emanuel Harmon was the owner of the property.

The Harmon Family

According to his death certificate, Emanuel Harmon[14] was born in Adams County, Pennsylvania, in about 1818. Evidently he later moved to Ohio.[15] In 1849 Harmon applied for a federal patent entitled "Improvements in Shading Pictures by Metallic Leaves."[16] Sometime between 1849 and 1855 he moved to Washington, D.C., where he resided during the Battle of Gettysburg.[17] While in Washington he received five more patents; three involving improvements on envelopes and postage, one entitled "Improvement in Stockings," and another labeled "Fireproof Iron Building." (The latter is somewhat ironic in that Harmon's Gettysburg home was put to the torch eight years later.)[18]

In 1857 Harmon purchased the 124-acre farm on Willoughby's Run that was occupied by apparent members of his family at the time of the battle.

Harmon died in February 1876 of Bright's disease of the kidney. "Intemperance" (alcohol) was a contributing factor in his death.

UNITED STATES PATENT OFFICE.

EMANUEL HARMON, OF CLEVELAND, OHIO.

IMPROVEMENT IN SHADING PICTURES BY METALLIC LEAVES.

Specification forming part of Letters Patent No. **6,241**, dated March 27, 1849.

To all whom it may concern:

Be it known that I, EMANUEL HARMON, of Cleveland, Cuyahoga county, and State of Ohio, have discovered a new method or process of taking miniatures of pictures of all kinds on glass by the means of gold, silver, platina, and copper-leaf, which I call the "Aureotypic Process," or "Celestial Painting;" and I hereby declare that the following is a full and exact description of the same.

First, a drawing is taken of the object to be represented. Secondly, a polished glass of the requisite dimensions is then gilded in any of the various modes of gilding glass which leaves the gilding pliable and brilliant, a gilding of the requisite pliability and brilliancy being thus obtained.

The outlines of the drawing, painting, engraving, or lithograph are taken in miniature by the pentagraph, a sharp metallic point being substituted for the pencil or other marking-instrument used in tracing maps and reducing figures and proportions.

The shading is transferred in the following manner: If the picture is principally in light or relievo, the lightest leaf, marked No. one, (1,) is to be used first in gilding. If the picture is mainly in perspective or shade, then the leaf No. two (2) is first used. If the picture is equally in light and shade, then either may be used first, at the election of the artist. The outlines of the lights or shades, as the case may be, are then first cut by the pentagraph and the leaf removed and light or dark leaf substituted, as required. Where slight shading is required, No. two (2) must be used. If deep shade is required, or leaf No. two (2) is to be shaded, then leaf No. three (3) is to be inserted.

To make the shading graceful and gradual, a fine needle is used to scratch the adjoining gilding, so as to intermix the metallic colors gradually. To make the greater contrast in the lights and shades, gold-leaf may be procured so mixed with silver as to give it a much lighter appearance than leaf No. one, (1,) or silver leaf itself, or platinum, or leaf by any means colored so as to retain its brilliancy may be used, and Nos. one (1) and two (2) for the shade. After the shading is completed the glass is put exactly in its former position, the outlines of the miniature then cut, and the superfluous leaf removed.

To protect the gilding it must be painted with a sort of japan made by melting gum-asphaltum and an equal quantity of spirits of turpentine. The miniature being seen from the opposite side of the glass reverses the picture. To prevent this, where it is material, the picture or object must be reversed in the first place.

The following is the process of casing: Another glass the size of the case is painted around the border with the japan, and before it is so dry as to become brittle a ruler and sharp point are used to mark out a sufficient space for the picture, and the japan within the lines must be removed by running a soft piece of wood slightly wet along the japanning, protecting the lines by a ruler, and the glass cleaned by a damp cloth. This glass is placed over the picture, which surrounds it with a halo and a beautiful background ; or a picture may be taken in a manner more like a painting by marking the outlines as described and covering them over with a deeper or different shade of leaf, the contrast serving to indicate the lines. In taking likenesses, in particular, the hair can be thus represented to advantage, and other features—indeed, the whole picture. Practice, good sense, and a good machine are all that is required to make a miniature perfectly correct, of unapproachable brilliancy and durability, either as ornaments or as devices for signs, &c.

The size of the miniature can be made of any desirable dimensions, depending upon the size of the picture and the size and compass of the pentagraph.

What I claim as my discovery, and desire to secure by Letters Patent, is—

The shading of gilded pictures by metallic leaves and by the process herein described.

EMANUEL HARMON.

Witnesses:
N. T. BOWLER,
J. HOLMES.

PATENT APPLICATION SUBMITTED BY EMANUEL HARMON FOR HIS "AUREOTYPIC PROCESS" (USPTO)

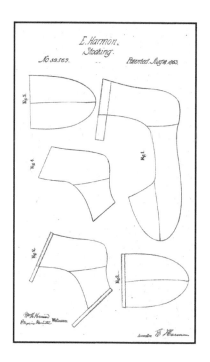

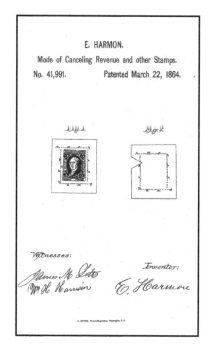

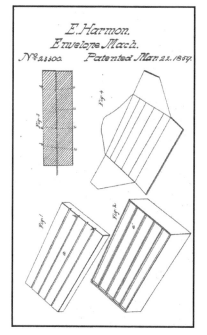

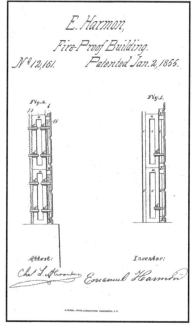

VARIOUS PATENT DRAWINGS BY EMANUEL HARMON (USPTO)

A longstanding mystery concerns the relationship of Emanuel Harmon to the 1863 tenants of his farm.

Amelia Evelyn Harmon was born in York County, Pennsylvania, to Dr. Richard Tyding Harmon and Amelia Jewell Camp.[19] Richard—known as R.T.—was a doctor of homeopathy, having attended the Homeopathic Medical College of Pennsylvania in Philadelphia.[20] He later married Amelia Camp of Louisiana; their daughter, Amelia, was born in December 1846.[21]

Amelia Harmon's mother died sometime before 1863. R.T. remarried, began a new family, and left Amelia with her grandparents.[22] Since they appear on the 1860 census adjacent to John Herbst, R.T. and his family must have occupied the Harmon house in 1860 but left before the battle.[23]

In 1852 a letter from R.T. Harmon appeared in the *Water Cure Journal*. In another issue, Harmon was listed among a group of "hydropathic" physicians from Ohio. This is somewhat ironic in that underground springs located on his family's property in Gettysburg later became famous for their curative powers.[24]

At the outbreak of the Civil War, Harmon enlisted in a Pennsylvania artillery battery. At the time of the Battle of Gettysburg, he was serving in Gen. Ulysses S. Grant's army.

With her father absent, Amelia was raised in Warrington Township, York County, by her grandparents, Abraham and Catherine Harmon.[25] Between 1860 and 1863 she moved to Gettysburg to live with her aunt and uncle, Rachel D. Harmon and David W. Finefrock, who were living on Emanuel Harmon's farm at the time.[26] Born in Maryland in about 1810, David Finefrock was a blacksmith by trade. Rachel Harmon was born in Pennsylvania in about 1828.[27]

William Comfort, a tenant famer, also lived on the Harmon property in 1863. He later married Mary P. Harmon, another of Amelia's aunts.[28]

After moving to Adams County, Amelia enrolled in Carrie Sheads's Oak Ridge Seminary, a school for young girls. In 1863 she was just 16; the Civil War had been raging for more than two years. Little did she realize that the fighting would shortly reach her doorstep.[29]

July 1863: Field of Battle

The Confederate Invasion

After resounding Confederate victories in Virginia, Robert E. Lee and his emboldened army were again headed north. In May and June of 1863, three sizable Confederate Army corps crossed into Pennsylvania through the Shenandoah Valley. At the same time, Gen. Joseph Hooker's bruised Army of the Potomac cautiously moved northward to intercept Lee and protect Washington. Yielding to mounting pressure, Hooker resigned and was replaced by Fifth Corps commander Gen. George G. Meade just three days before the two armies clashed at Gettysburg.

On June 26 Gettysburg residents were shocked to find the town occupied by Confederate soldiers of Gen. Jubal Early's division. Several days later two brigades of Gen. John Buford's Union cavalry were cheered into Gettysburg. The troopers had just missed Gen. James J. Pettigrew's Confederate brigade, which had moved eastward toward Gettysburg on the Chambersburg Pike in search of supplies. After crossing Herr's Ridge, the Confederates discontinued their march.

Buford immediately set up a network of pickets to cover all the major roads that pass through Gettysburg. As night fell he sent word to the nearest Union corps commander, Gen. John F. Reynolds, briefing him on what he knew of the enemy's whereabouts.

Early on the morning of July 1, 1863, two Rebel divisions of Gen. A.P. Hill's corps moved along the Chambersburg Pike toward Gettysburg. Just before crossing Marsh Creek they were fired upon by Buford's advanced skirmishers of the 8th Illinois Cavalry. The deadliest battle of the American Civil War had begun.

Years later Amelia Harmon remembered that terrifying morning:

> We were living on the tragic morning of the battle in the big colonial
> mansion known as the "Old McLean Place" situated on the highest

point of the bluff overlooking Willoughby's Run. We had decided to remain in the house even in the uncertain event of a battle, although most of our neighbors had abandoned their homes, for ours was of the old-fashioned fortress type with 18-inch walls and heavy wooden shutters. My aunt and I, then but a school girl, were quite alone, our farmer having gone away with the horses in the hope of hiding them in the fastness of the hills. At nine A.M. on the morning of July 1 came the ominous boom of a cannon to the west of us. We rushed to the window to behold hundreds of galloping horses coming up the road, through the fields and even past our very door. Boom! Again spoke the cannon, more and more galloping horses, their excited riders shouting and yelling to each other and pushing westward in hot haste, past the house and the barn, seeking the shelter of a strip of woods on the ridge beyond. But the ridge was alive with the enemy! A few warning shots from its cover sent them flying back to find shelter behind the barn, outbuildings, trees, and even the pump, seeking to hold the enemy in check. We did not know it then but were in the very center of the first shock of the battle between Hill's forces and the advance line of Buford's Cavalry. Horses and men were falling under our eyes by shots from an unseen foe, and the confusion became greater every minute. Filled with alarm and terror we locked all the doors and rushed to the second floor—and threw open the shutters of the west window. One glance only and a half-spent minnie ball from the woods crashed into the shutter close to my aunt's ear leaving but the thickness of paper between her and death. This one glance showed us that a large timothy field between the barn and the woods concealed hundreds of gray crouching figures stealthily advancing under its cover, and picking off every cavalryman who appeared for an instant in sight. An officer's horse just under the window was shot and the officer fell to the ground. "Look—" we fairly shrieked to him, "the field is full of Rebels." "Leave the window," he shouted in return, "or you'll be killed!" We needed no second warning and rushed to the cupola. Here the whole landscape for miles around unrolled like a panorama below us. What a spectacle! It seemed as though the fields and woods had been sown with dragon's teeth, for everywhere had sprung up armed men, where but an hour ago only grass and flowers grew.[30]

Archer's Misfortune

The skirmishers Amelia referred to were likely men of the 8th New York Cavalry, Companies B and F. These troopers were among the first to engage Gen. Henry Heth's division of rebels as they approached Gettysburg. According to Col. William L. Markell of the 8th New York, his men were "fighting stubbornly...behind fences and trees."[31] As pressure mounted, additional reinforcements were rushed to the skirmish line, and a sharp fight ensued between Archer's men and the cavalrymen. Several casualties were sustained during this early stage of the battle.

Meanwhile, Gen. James J. Archer's Rebel brigade deployed in the northern half of the Springs Hotel Woods. These battle-hardened veterans had led the march to Gettysburg that morning. Although he commanded a brigade of Tennessee and Alabama men, Archer was by no means a southerner, having been born in Maryland during the 1820s. A member of his brigade described him this way:

GEN. JAMES J. ARCHER (USAMHI)

His exterior was rough and unattractive, small of stature and angular of feature, his temper was irascible and so cold was his manner that we thought him at first a Martinet [a strict disciplinarian]. Very noncommunicative, and the bearing and extreme reserve of the old army officer made him, for a time, one of the most intensely hated of men. No sooner, however, had he led his brigade through the first Richmond campaign, than quite a revolution took place in sentiment.... Beneath his rough exterior beat a warm heart. But his estimate of men was always from the standard of a soldier. His judgment of them was infallible. For some officers he had a contempt, while there were privates for whom he never failed a warm hand-shake. He had none of the politician or aristocrat, but he never lost the dignity or bearing of an officer. While in battle he seemed the very God of War, and every inch a soldier according to its strictest rules, but when the humblest private approached his quarters he was courteous. There was no deception in him and he spoke his mind freely, but always with the severest dignity. He won the hearts of his men by his wonderful judgment and conduct on the field, and they had the most implicit confidence in him.... He was held in the highest regard by General Harry Heth, A.P. Hill, and Stonewall Jackson. He was devoted to his brigade, and refused a major general's commission rather than be separated from this brigade.[32]

At this time the majority of Archer's brigade moved into the woods to escape deadly artillery fire from Lt. John H. Calef's battery on McPherson's Ridge.[33] Archer's regiments were most likely deployed in the following order: 7th Tennessee, 14th Tennessee, 13th Alabama, 1st Tennessee.[34] The 5th Alabama Battalion and a detachment of the 13th Alabama acted as the brigade's skirmish line. Sometime during the advance, Maj. A.S. Van de Graaff, commanding the 5th Alabama Battalion, was covered with dirt after one of Calef's shells exploded at his feet.[35]

According to W.H. Moon of the 13th Alabama, a Confederate battery moved forward and hurled projectiles at the Federals from a position on the right front of his regiment. From here Moon had a clear view of the field of advance across the Harmon farm: "an open field which extended down to and across Willoughby Run...a gradual slope with a dip about one hundred and fifty yards from the run."[36] Lt. Col. Samuel G. Shepard, 7th Tennessee, also described the terrain: "At the extreme side of the field there was a small creek with a fence and undergrowth."[37]

Shortly thereafter Archer and his brigade moved out of the Springs Hotel Woods in line of battle.

As the rebels approached Willoughby's Run, they came under heavier artillery fire. One Confederate described this as a "shower of shells."[38] This came mostly from a section of Calef's 2nd United States Light Artillery, Battery A, that had been posted along what is now Reynolds Avenue. It was commanded by Sgt. Charles Pergel. While riding to this position, Calef witnessed the Confederate advance:

> It was Archer's brigade, and their battle-flags looked redder and bloodier in the strong July sun than I had ever seen them before. At those flags the firing was directed, and my gunners succeeded in making excellent shots, throwing the lines into some confusion.[39]

While under fire from Calef's guns, Archer's line was still being harassed by elements of the 8th New York Cavalry. Despite all this, the Rebels continued across the Harmon farm toward Herbst Woods.[40]

W.H. Moon, 13th Alabama, described an interesting incident:

> I was color guard on the left of the color bearer, Tom Grant. He was a big, double-jointed six-footer...he was waving the flag and holloaing at the top of his voice, making a fine target while the shells were flying thick around us. I said: "Tom, if you don't stop that I will use my bayonet on you." Just then a fusillade of rifle balls from the Federals greeted us, and Tom needed no further admonition from me.[41]

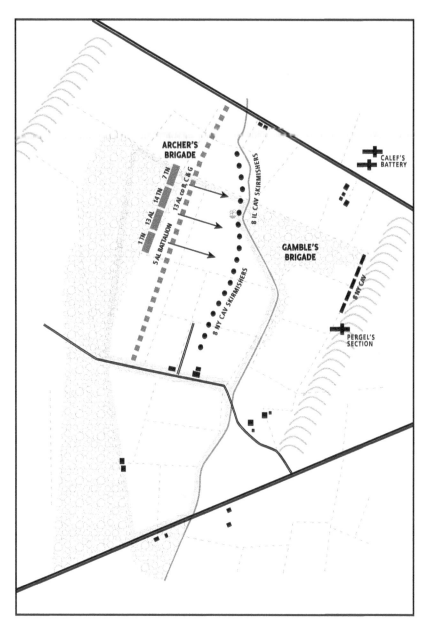

ARCHER'S ADVANCE ACROSS THE HARMON FARM

Archer's brigade then halted at Willoughby's Run for a short time to reform and reload. At this position, an abrupt rise east of the creek protected the rebels from artillery fire. This elevation exists today and can be seen clearly because of a recent tree-removal project near the 19th Indiana monument. After this brief respite, Archer's brigade renewed its attack and "rushed across [Willoughby's Run] with a cheer."[42]

The arrival at this juncture of Gen. Solomon Meredith's famed "Iron Brigade" likely saved McPherson's Ridge for the Army of the Potomac.[43] From her vantage point in the cupola of the Harmon house, Amelia witnessed the sharp clash that ensued. Many years later she wrote:

> Soon we saw a strong detachment of Rebels file out from the fringe of woods, a quarter of a mile distant to meet a body of Federals advancing rapidly from the direction of the town and in a few moments we were witnessing the quick, sharp engagement in which Gen. Reynolds fell. Hardly was this ended, when we observed a dark, sinuous line winding around the distant hills beyond the town, like a huge serpent. It was Meade's army advancing on the double quick to the relief of Reynolds.[44]

Not long after the initial clash, Archer's men were overwhelmed by westerners of the Iron Brigade and forced back across Willoughby's Run. This was primarily due to an attack by the 19th Indiana and 24th Michigan on the Confederate right flank. In addition to being forced to withdraw, many men of the 1st Tennessee and 13th Alabama were unable to escape and were forced to surrender. This was due in part to the presence of Willoughby's Run in their rear. One rebel estimated that 75 men of the brigade were captured, although the actual number was surely much higher.[45] Archer himself was among those captured, taken by Pvt. Patrick Maloney, Company G, 2nd Wisconsin, "about 30 paces west of Willoughby's Run."[46] Dennis B. Daily of the 2nd Wisconsin, who quickly arrived on the scene, wrote:

> Archer at first resisted arrest, but soon Maloney had help, and the sullen general was subdued. When I arrived on the spot, Gen. Archer appealed to me for protection from Maloney. I then requested him to give me his sword and belt, which he did with great reluctance, saying that courtesy permitted him to retain his side arms.[47]

Lt. Col. S. G. Shepard, 7th Tennessee, wrote that he "saw General Archer a short time before he surrendered, and he appeared to be very much exhausted with fatigue."[48] One account relates that Archer was captured while seeking refuge in a clump of willows. Post-battle maps indicate that this small grove was located in close proximity to what would later become the famous Katalysine Spring.[49]

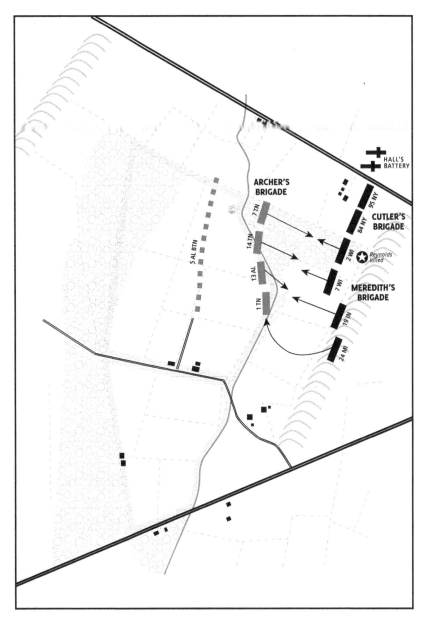

ARCHER'S ATTACK ACROSS WILLOUGHBY'S RUN

Meanwhile, the attack continued on Archer's right flank. Col. Henry A. Morrow's 24th Michigan pushed across the creek, where his men captured scores of Tennesseans.[50] Capt. J.B. Turney of the 1st Tennessee barely escaped capture himself: "I dropped on my knees, and, looking beneath the hanging smoke, saw the feet and legs of the enemy...."[51]

Amidst the confusion, some soldiers in the 13th Alabama were unaware of the desperate situations on both flanks. W.H. Moon wrote: "We were rather enjoying the fray when an order was given to 'fall back on Willoughby Run.' We could see no reason for the order...."[52]

W.H. Bird of the 13th Alabama had a very different experience:

> ... all of a sudden a heavy line of battle rose up out of the wheat, and poured a volley into our ranks, it wavered and they charged us, and we fell back to the ravine again, and before we could possibly rally, it seemed to me there were 20,000 Yanks down in among us hollowing [*sic*] surrender... the Lieutenant looked at me and said: Bird, what in the h—ll shall I do? I remarked, I don't see what you can do, but surrender, and he threw down his sword.[53]

Though many of his comrades were pinned down at the ravine, W.A. Castleberry of the 13th Alabama was able to reach the safety of the Springs Hotel Woods where for the next several hours he watched in horror as the two massive armies concentrated on the battlefield.

Perhaps Lt. Col. Shepard of the 7th Tennessee best summarized the retreat:

> Being completely overpowered by numbers, and our support not being near enough to give us any assistance, we fell back across the field, and reformed just in rear of the brigade that had started in as our support.[54]

Clearly, the attack could be considered bad luck, as many of Archer's men believed that they were fighting only pesky local militia. In fact, they were in a bloody struggle with crack troops of the Army of the Potomac.

Meanwhile Col. John M. Brockenbrough's small Virginia brigade arrived on the field. Its four regiments had marched to Gettysburg behind the brigades of Archer and Davis that morning. Brockenbrough immediately deployed his men south of the Chambersburg Pike and advanced through the Springs Hotel Woods. His regiments were likely arranged in the following order from left to right: 55th Virginia, 47th Virginia, 40th Virginia, 22nd Virginia Battalion.[55] Col. Robert M. Mayo of the 47th Virginia recalled:

> On arriving in the second body of woods from the town, we ascertained from the rapid firing that Archer's Brigade was engaged in

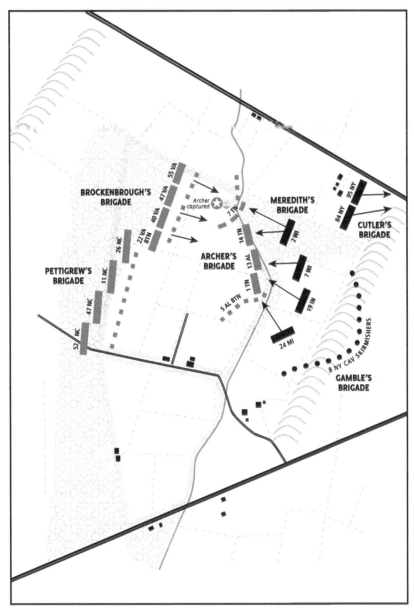

BROCKENBROUGH'S
BRIGADE

55 VA
47 VA
40 VA
22 VA BTN
26 NC

Archer
captured

7 TN

14 TN

13 AL

1 TN

5 AL BTN

ARCHER'S
BRIGADE

MEREDITH'S
BRIGADE

2 WI

7 WI

19 IN

24 MI

95 NY

84 NY

CUTLER'S
BRIGADE

8 NY CAV SKIRMISHERS

GAMBLE'S
BRIGADE

PETTIGREW'S
BRIGADE

11 NC
47 NC
52 NC

ARCHER'S RETREAT AND THE ARRIVAL OF PETTIGREW AND BROCKENBROUGH ON THE FIELD

21

a sharp encounter with the enemy, in the woods nearest the town, and we were hurried forward to its assistance but on arriving near the stream running along the edge of the woods, we found his men falling back, having been outflanked and overpowered by numbers. Finding that the enemy's force out flanked us for at least half a mile on each side, Col. Brockenbrough withdrew his Brigade about 150 yards to the second body of woods, and awaited reinforcements, we remained in this position several hours.[56]

According to a rebel chaplain, before Brockenbrough's men retired from their advanced position near Willoughby's Run "Brockenbrough, also in marching order, ordered 'left-face, load;' then, unable to fire because of the flying Tennesseans, he back-stepped the brigade until in line with Davis'[s] Brigade." The Virginians then returned to the Springs Hotel Woods to await a second order to advance.[57]

After their climactic attack and defeat of Archer's brigade, the rest of the Iron Brigade pushed across Willoughby's Run to pursue fleeing Confederates. Evidently several Union casualties were sustained during this movement onto the Harmon farm:

> The Twenty-fourth Michigan was on the extreme left of the Iron Brigade during the charge, and swept over the hill, down across Willoughby Run, swinging clear around the ravine in which was Archer's forces, most of whom were thus captured with General Archer himself. It was a victory indeed, but at the cost of precious lives, including its valiant color-bearer, Sergeant Abel G. Peck. The regiment then about-faced and drove the uncaptured foe over the crest and a hundred yards beyond....[58]

The "crest" occupied by the 24th Michigan was a small ridge between the Springs Hotel Woods and Willoughby's Run. The Harmon farm buildings stood on this ridge southwest of the regiment's position, and they did not escape the notice of Col. Henry A. Morrow: "After advancing to the crest of the hill beyond the run, we were halted, and threw out skirmishers to the front and also to the left, near a brick house."[59]

COL. HENRY A. MORROW (LOC)

The 19th Indiana also occupied this advanced position. Col. Samuel J. Williams ordered his men across the creek to the Harmon farm.[60]

On the right of the brigade the 2nd and 7th Wisconsin quickly joined their sister regiments on the west bank of the stream. Lt. Col. John B. Callis of the 7th described

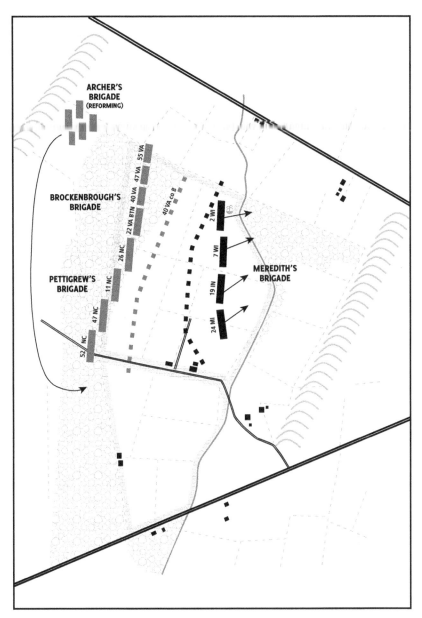

THE IRON BRIGADE'S ADVANCED POSITION ON THE HARMON FARM

the situation: "I beheld a line of the enemy either end of which I could not see and but a short distance from us, they commenced sending out skirmishers."[61] After capturing Gen. Archer, the 2nd Wisconsin formed a line on the Harmon farm facing west. It was here that Pvt. Jonathan R. Bryan of Company H met a terrible fate: "[he] was shot through the heart by a Confederate from the edge of the woods beyond a field in our front, while waving his hat and cheering for victory." Bryan was apparently the only member of the 2nd Wisconsin to be killed west of Willoughby's Run. The Confederate who killed him was probably a retreating Tennessean of Archer's brigade or one of Brockenbrough's newly arrived Virginians.[62]

The presence of fresh Confederate infantry on the field quickly made the Iron Brigade's position on the Harmon farm untenable, necessitating a withdrawal to Herbst Woods. Gen. James J. Pettigrew's large force of North Carolinians posed an especially dangerous threat. An aide to Gen. Solomon Meredith soon arrived on the Harmon farm with orders to fall back. During this movement, Lt. Col. Mark Flanigan, 24th Michigan, was severely wounded in his leg, which was later amputated. Nearby, Adjutant William H. Rexford was struck in the groin.[63] The regiments of the brigade assumed new positions upon their withdrawal to Herbst Woods, from left to right: 19th Indiana, 24th Michigan, 2nd Wisconsin, 7th Wisconsin.[64] Skirmishers were immediately thrown out from the various regiments, taking position along the banks of Willoughby's Run, protected by dense shrubbery and underbrush.

Midday Lull

Comprising some of the largest regiments in the Rebel army, Gen. James J. Pettigrew's North Carolina brigade was a force to be reckoned with. After arriving on Herr's Ridge, the brigade initially took position north of the Chambersburg Pike, but was soon moved to the fields around the Herr Tavern. The Tar Heels waited in this position until ordered forward, halting again in the Springs Hotel Woods near present-day Country Club Lane. The units of the brigade were positioned from left to right: 26th North Carolina, 11th North Carolina, 47th North Carolina, 52nd North Carolina.[65] On Pettigrew's left, Brockenbrough's Virginians also waited under cover of the trees. Pettigrew's regiments were so large that, according to some accounts, they were "in line by echelon, the Twenty-sixth being in advance and the Eleventh on its right some distance in the rear; the Forty-seventh regiment in rear of the Eleventh, and the Fifty-second in rear of the Forty-seventh."[66] Pettigrew's flank probably

GEN. JAMES J. PETTIGREW (LOOMC)

rested somewhere near where the Mill Road passes through the Springs Hotel Woods.[67] Maj. John T. Jones, 26th North Carolina, recalled:

> In our front was a wheat-field about a fourth of a mile wide; then came a branch, with thick underbrush and briars skirting the banks. Beyond this was again an open field, with the exception of a wooded hill directly in front of the Twenty-sixth Regiment, about covering its front.[68]

MAJ. JOHN T. JONES (HSABNC)

Skirmishers from the brigade were then thrown out, as witnessed by the officers and men of the Iron Brigade.

Meanwhile, remnants of Archer's brigade reformed west of the Springs Hotel Woods. Col. Birkett D. Fry of the 13th Alabama was left in command of the brigade. After the five battered regiments regrouped and reformed, they were ordered to a position on Pettigrew's right. W.M. McCall, 7th Tennessee, remembered: "...the entire brigade was sent over to the extreme right of Lee's Army to watch the Federal cavalry threatening that point and remained there all day...."[69]

COL. BIRKETT D. FRY (PHOTCW)

In this position, somewhere between the Mill Road and the Fairfield Road, the brigade awaited further orders. Soon after, Capt. J.B. Turney's Company K of the 1st Tennessee was ordered forward as skirmishers.[70]

On Fry's right flank was the 8th Illinois Cavalry. Best known for firing the first shots of the battle, the regiment played a much more important role during the afternoon attacks. Upon being relieved by units of the first corps, the men were sent to a position on the Fairfield Road where they threatened Heth's right flank. Maj. John L. Beveridge, who commanded the unit at Gettysburg, remembered that they deployed in an orchard near the southern extension of the Spring Hotel Woods.[71]

According to post-battle maps, this was the Henry Meals orchard. Just west of the orchard, a small farm lane led south from the Fairfield Road. Col. Chapman Biddle's brigade later used this road to reach the field.[72] Most of the Illinois cavalrymen were posted in the orchard, with some troopers occupying the woods north of the road and others in the fields between the road and the John Herbst house. The steep western banks of Willoughby's Run likely concealed these cavalrymen from members of Heth's division. From this position the 8th Illinois would aid Union infantry during the upcoming Confederate attacks.

Marcellus Jones, a member of the regiment, wrote: "[we] occupied the woods north of the Fairfield Road most of the afternoon, with one squadron on picket further out on the road and in the open ground to the west."[73] This single squadron may have been responsible for saving a small detachment of the Eleventh Corps that was wandering toward the battlefield from the direction of Fairfield. About one hundred Ohioans of Adelbert Ames's brigade had been sent toward Fountaindale, Pennsylvania, that morning "as the enemy was reported to be in that neighborhood." Before arriving there they heard gunfire and were immediately ordered to move toward Gettysburg by way of the Fairfield Road. The Federal officer in charge of this force wrote:

MAJ. JOHN L. BEVERIDGE (USAMHI)

I had a good map of the country and as we reached the place the conflict was distinctly heard. I came in between the two Cavalry picket lines, and fortunately was first discovered by our men. They distinguished us by the uniforms and before I got sight of them; when one came down the road on horse and said: "Where in ---- did you come from? Don't you know the Johnnies are right over there?" I had been advancing with care, a few men ahead with instructions which direction to take, in the event we were attacked. We made little time in reaching our pickets, followed them as I remember across the field about where Pickett's charge was made ... gaining the Emmitsburg road leading in the town; we went through it and met our Brigade....[74]

The 8th Illinois was also responsible for covering an entire Union brigade as they approached the field. Col. Chapman Biddle's brigade of the Union First Corps had taken a different road to Gettysburg on the morning of July 1. Instead of moving north on the Emmitsburg Road with the rest of the First Corps, they crossed Marsh Creek and traveled north toward the Fairfield Road, eventually arriving along the lines of the 8th Illinois Cavalry near the Meals orchard.[75] Capt. John Cook, 20th New York State Militia (80th New York), remembered:

COL. CHAPMAN BIDDLE (12thPV)

A little after nine o'clock we turned out from the

road into a woods pasture, a beautiful grove of large trees with a carpet of springy sod. Here we were drawn up in line to form the left wing of the corps. For a short time we enjoyed the cool shade and quiet of the position.[76]

A member of the 121st Pennsylvania also recalled arriving at this spot:

[we] came out on the Hagerstown Road, on the crest of a slight ridge west of Gettysburg, among the Eighth Illinois Cavalry. The enemy's line was clearly seen about 1,000 yards to the west, extending out of a wood into an open field where the men were lying down.[77]

At this point Biddle's brigade began to advance into the Springs Hotel Woods. However, the presence of Confederates ahead forced Biddle to cut east toward town across the Stallsmith farm. The course of the first day's battle would surely have been different had these men continued through the woods. Heth's entire division would have been flanked.[78]

Capt. Cook of the 20th New York State Militia recalled an incident that occurred after his regiment moved out of the woods toward Willoughby's Run:

...one of the men fell suddenly, stricken down by a stray bullet from the forest. Our surgeon leaped from his horse and ran to help the wounded man, and as we swept past in hurrying march we had an impressive intimation of what was to come. The incident thrilled every one with a sense of danger as great perhaps as that felt during the battle itself.[79]

The brigade moved quickly in column formation toward Willoughby's Run and crossed near the Harmon farmhouse. Before they reached the creek, Biddle's entourage was spotted by Union soldiers positioned on McPherson's Ridge. One soldier wrote, "[Rowley's] advanced guard had arrived on the field and was near the woods and the road, about where the brick house and the barn were burned." Biddle's men crossed the creek near where the Mill Road passed through it. Because there was likely no bridge there at the time, the water must have been particularly shallow at that point.[80]

Shortly thereafter the brigade arrived on McPherson's Ridge, taking position on its eastern slope. Biddle's men were then moved forward and stopped temporarily along the east bank of Willoughby's Run.

Meanwhile, after pushing dismounted cavalry out of their way, Pettigrew's skirmishers gained the slight ridge at the Harmon farmhouse and threatened Biddle's position at the creek. Col. Theodore B. Gates wrote:

Along the top of the ridge on the opposite side of the Run was a

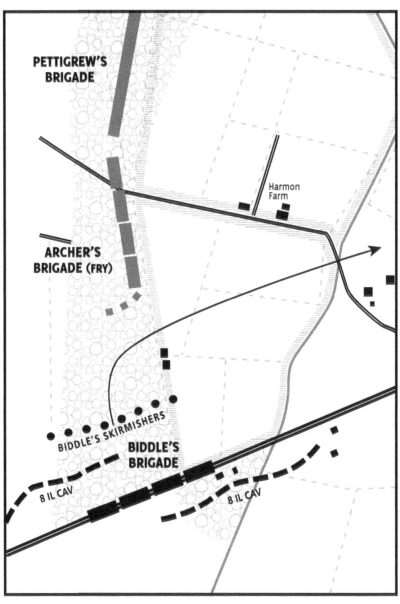

PETTIGREW'S
BRIGADE

ARCHER'S
BRIGADE (FRY)

Harmon
Farm

BIDDLE'S SKIRMISHERS

BIDDLE'S
BRIGADE

8 IL CAV

8 IL CAV

THE ROUTE OF COL. CHAPMAN BIDDLE'S BRIGADE ACROSS THE STALLSMITH FARM

fence, and the field beyond it was covered with grain, affording excellent shelter for the enemy's sharpshooters, and the field was alive with them. In this ravine the brigade found itself under a hot infantry fire, and was unable to see the enemy from whom the fire came, and did not attempt to reply to it....[81]

COL. THEODORE B. GATES (LOC)

Because of the vulnerability of the low ground around Willoughby's' Run, Biddle's brigade was ordered to withdraw to McPherson's Ridge. However, not all the regiments occupied the crest. Col. Gates suggested that his 20th New York State Militia was the only regiment to do so.[82]

Fight for the Harmon House

For Col. Chapman Biddle's brigade, the first half hour on McPherson's Ridge had been unpleasant. Enos Vail remembered:

> ...we were greatly annoyed by a company of sharpshooters who had taken possession of a house in front of us and were killing and wounding many of our men. Their fire was very destructive among the gunners of Cooper's Battery which we were supporting. The gunners were picked off so fast that some of our men had to assist them to work the guns.[83]

Gen. James S. Wadsworth must have noticed the effects of this fire on Biddle's line. He immediately rode up to Col. Gates and directed him to send a company of his regiment to take the Harmon house. Capt. Cook recalled: "General Wadsworth, who had been our first brigade commander and was then with the next division of the corps, had recommended us for the duty; that he knew our regiment would go where it was sent and stay where it was put."[84]

Union accounts indicate that some of the Confederate skirmishers, probably members of Pettigrew's brigade, were inside the Harmon barn. Col. Chapman Biddle wrote: "Upwards of three-quarters of a mile in front were woods nearly parallel with the line of battle and between, somewhat to the left, a house and a large stone barn, the latter of which was...used as a cover for the enemy's sharpshooters."[85]

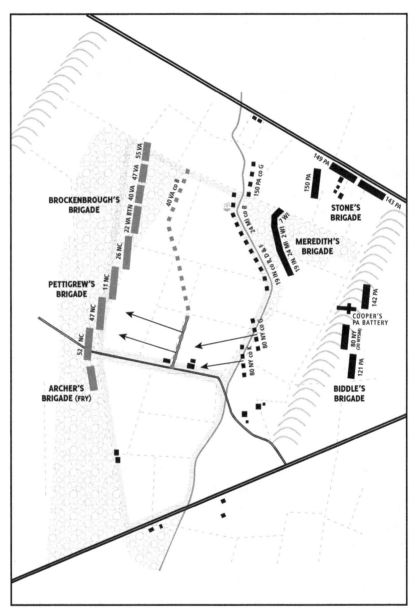

MEN OF THE 20TH NEW YORK STATE MILITIA CAPTURE THE HARMON HOUSE FROM PETTIGREW'S SKIRMISHERS. (THE ARRIVAL OF COMPANY G OF THE 20TH NYSM WAS NEARLY AN HOUR LATER THAN THE ARRIVAL OF COMPANY K.)

Enos Vail detailed the frightful capabilities of the Confederate skirmishers in a post-battle recollection:

> ...the wounds that put the entire Color Guard out of the fight came from that building. Sergeant Beckett, who carried the national color, lost the fingers from one of his hands, and John and I were soon on the ground to take his place. The eagle was shot from the top of the flag-staff which Beckett carried. It was found on the field, and subsequently recovered. This all occurred within twenty minutes of the beginning of the battle.[86]

Col. Gates was quick to detach Capt. Ambrose N. Baldwin and the men of Company K, who steadily crossed the Herbst farm and made their way toward Willoughby's Run. Historian and 20th New York State Militia expert Seward R. Osborne calculated that there were merely 38 men in this company at the time of the battle.[87]

According to Enos Vail, additional soldiers joined the men of Company K. Pvt. Alexander Tice of Company E was apparently among them. Before the battle, Tice had told Vail: "You know that I have never been in battle, and I have a presentiment that I am going to be killed." His premonition proved to be true.[88]

CAPT. AMBROSE N. BALDWIN (SROC)

While under fire, Baldwin led his small force of New Yorkers across Willoughby's Run and up the steep west bank of the ravine. After what was described as a "spirited contest," Baldwin and his men prevailed by driving Pettigrew's skirmishers back. During this clash, Pvt. Tice was killed not far from the Harmon house. Enos Vail recalled, "Feeling as he did that his last day had come, he voluntarily went forward to certain death, which required a vast amount of courage." Tice was later buried in the Gettysburg National Cemetery beside his fallen comrades.[89]

Years later Amelia Harmon vividly described the arrival of Company K at her doorstep:

> A sudden, violent commotion and uproar below made us fly in quick haste to the lower floor. There was a tumultuous pounding with fists and guns on the kitchen door and loud yells of "Open, or we'll break down the doors." Which they proceeded to do. We drew the bolt and in poured a stream of maddened, powder blackened blue coats, who ordered us to the cellar, while they dispersed to the various west

windows throughout the house. From our cellar prison we could hear the tumult above, the constant crack of rifles, the hurried orders, and outside the mingled roar of heavy musketry, galloping horses, yelling troops and the occasional boom of cannon to the westward. The suspense and agony of uncertainty were awful! We could hear the beating of our own hearts above all the wild confusion. How long this lasted I know not.[90]

The tables had turned on Pettigrew's North Carolinians, who were now targets for Baldwin's skirmishers. At this time, Col. James K. Marshall's 52nd North Carolina was positioned near the Mill Road in the Springs Hotel Woods, directly west of the Harmon house. A member of the regiment noted that much of this destructive fire came from the second story windows of the Harmon house.[91]

Col. George H. Faribault's 47th North Carolina was also bothered by this incessant sharpshooting. J. Rowan Rogers remembered:

> ...after our line was formed we were ordered to halt, and as the enemy was keeping up a rather hot fire upon our main line, skirmishers from our regiment were ordered to advance and drive them back out of reach of our line, which was done, but not until several of our regiment were wounded and our gallant Lieutenant-Colonel, John A. Graves, was slightly wounded on the leg, the ball first having hit the iron scabbard of his sword, which was hanging by his side.[92]

Meanwhile, on the left of the brigade, Col. Henry K. Burgwyn, Jr., 26th North Carolina, "became quite impatient to engage the enemy." He knew that precious time was being lost as Union reinforcements streamed onto the fields west of town. Lt. Col. John R. Lane wrote of the young colonel: "...his eye was aflame with the ardor for battle." Just twenty-one years of age, Burgwyn would later become known as "the boy colonel."[93]

A member of the 26th North Carolina also remembered the pesky Federal skirmishers at the Harmon house:

> While we were still lying down impatiently waiting to begin the engagement, the right of the regiment was greatly annoyed by some sharpshooters stationed on the top of a large old farm house to our right. Col. Burgwyn ordered a man sent forward to take them down,

COL. JAMES K. MARSHALL (VMI)

when Lieutenant J.A. Lowe, of Company G, volunteered. Creeping forward along a fence until he got a position from which he could see the men behind the chimney who were doing the shooting, he soon silenced them.[94]

After Lowe returned from his advanced position, firing continued. Another soldier wrote: "the enemy's sharpshooters occasionally reminded us that we had better cling close to the bosom of old mother earth." During their time in the woods, "many words of encouragement were spoken and some jokes were indulged in. Religious services were not held, as they should have been, owing to the absence of our Chaplains."[95]

During this lull, Burgwyn and Lane had the following conversation:

> Lieutenant Colonel Lane, who had been up all the night previous in charge of the division skirmish line, and had eaten but little, but had drunken freely of muddy water, was seized with an intolerable nausea and vomiting. Colonel Lane thus speaks of the incident: "I asked permission of Colonel Burgwyn to go to the rear. The latter replied: 'Oh, Colonel, I can't I can't, I can't think of going into this battle without you; here is a little of the best French brandy which my parents gave me to take with me in the battle; it may do you good." I took a little of it under the circumstances, though I had not drunk any during the war, and I may add, neither had Colonel Burgwyn. In a few minutes I was somewhat relieved and said: "Colonel Burgwyn, I can go with you." With his usual politeness, he replied: "Thank you, Colonel, thank you." Continuing the conversation, he said: "Colonel, do you think that we will have to advance on the enemy as they are? ... He saw and realized the very decided advantage their position gave them over us."[96]

Meanwhile, at the Harmon house pressure was mounting for Baldwin's Company K. According to historian Seward R. Osborne, Pvt. Addison S. Hayes was wounded in the right arm (necessitating amputation) while at the house. It is probable that more casualties were sustained at the Harmon house than were reported. Not long after, Capt. Baldwin sent his lieutenant, Jack Young, to the regiment's main line on McPherson's Ridge to request support. Capt. Cook of the 20th New York State Militia remembered:

COL. HENRY K. BURGWYN, JR. (HSBBNC)

As an officer [Young] had but one fault. He would get drunk and when drunk was riotous. There was a verse of a bawdy ballad. Which, when in that condition, he used to sing, or, rather, shout with the voice of a Stentor. He had been put in arrest for an escapade as we passed through Washington, but at his earnest petition had been released to share in the action. He was too good a man in a fight to be left out. The excitement acted on him like a stimulant, and as he came up along the front of the line of men lying down almost rigidly nervous under the prolonged exposure, with shot and shell whistling around him, he roared out the utterly unrepeatable verse of his favorite ballad at the top of his voice, and, raising his cap and wiping his heated face, shouted, "Col., it's d—d hot out there." The whole line broke into a roar of laughter, and the cool insouciance of Jack did more to relieve the mental strain which the long waiting under fire had caused than anything else could have done.[97]

PVT. ADDISON HAYES (SROC)

Despite the humorous nature of Young's request, Col. Gates understood the gravity of the situation and quickly sent Capt. William H. Cunningham's Company G to the Harmon farm. Pettigrew's forces were multiplying around the Harmon house.[98]

Afternoon Attacks

By mid-afternoon the order to attack finally reached Heth's division. Pettigrew's North Carolinians and Brockenbrough's Virginians crept forward, flanked by battered remnants of Archer's and Davis's brigades. Just south of the Chambersburg Pike, Brockenbrough's Virginians stepped out of the northern end of the Springs Hotel Woods and moved across the open fields of the Harmon farm. According to one account, the Virginians charged "rapidly upon the enemy whose right rested at the stone barn near the Rail Road."[99] Unfortunately, there are few accounts from Brockenbrough's brigade. Union infantry of Col. Roy Stone's Bucktail Brigade provided better eyewitness accounts than the Virginians themselves.[100] Maj. Thomas Chamberlain of the 150th Pennsylvania wrote that the Confederates were "descending rapidly towards Willoughby run—regiment upon regiment *en echelon*—followed by supporting columns, extending southward from the Chambersburg road as far as the eye could reach."[101] The rebels soon moved across Willoughby's Run and began to ascend McPherson's Ridge cautiously, moderating their movement "as if awaiting developments on other portions of the field." Once at the top of a quarry on the McPherson farm, Brockenbrough's regiments were in range of the 150th Pennsylvania. The Pennsylvanians and Virginians exchanged volley after volley, creating a "hail-storm," according to Maj. Chamberlain. Then the Virginians suddenly "ceased firing, fell back a short distance, and obliquing to their right were soon hidden from view by the woods."[102] (The reputation of Brockenbrough's brigade in the Army of Northern Virginia was not particularly good. The following year, division commander Henry Heth requested that the 22nd Virginia Battalion be broken up and distributed to the other brigades in the division. He wrote: "This Battalion on every battle field, from Gettysburg up until the present time has behaved in a most disgraceful manner.")[103]

CAPT. WILLIAM H. CUNNINGHAM (SROC)

Gen. Alfred Scales's brigade (of Pender's division) passed over Brockenbrough's line later that day. Scales wrote: "[we] came upon the front line, halted and lying down...the officers on this part of the line informed me that they were without ammunition, and would not advance farther. I immediately ordered my brigade to advance. We passed over them, up the ascent...." Meanwhile, the right half of Brockenbrough's line engaged part of the Iron Brigade but made little progress. Maj. John Mansfield, 2nd Wisconsin, reported that his skirmishers were engaged "with great spirit" but did not describe heavy fighting in his regiment's direct front.[104]

Simultaneously with this advance, the men of the 26th North Carolina had risen to their feet, many of them for the last time. A member of the regiment wrote:

> Suddenly there came down the line the long awaited command 'Attention.' The time of this command could not have been more inopportune; for our line had inspected the enemy and we well knew the desperateness of the charge we were to make; but with the greatest quickness the regiment obeyed.[105]

With over 800 guns glistening in the afternoon sun, the regiment stepped out from the Springs Hotel Woods into view of their enemies on McPherson's Ridge. Col. Burgwyn took his place in the center of the regiment, with Lt. Col. Lane on the right and Maj. Jones on the left. J.H. Mansfield, the colorbearer, stood near Burgwyn. The attack then commenced, and Col. Burgwyn was seen riding "gallantly along the line,"cheering his men forward.[106]

A *Confederate Veteran Magazine* article written after the war detailed the 26th North Carolina's advance across the Harmon farm:

...not many steps are taken until the enemy opens fire on them, and you observe men falling here and there. Several are killed and wounded; two of Company E have fallen; one of them is dead. The men are keeping step, and the line is as pretty and perfect as a regiment ever made...Look! The brave color bearer, Mansfield, is on his knees and the colors on the ground! Has he stumbled over that rock? No. He is wounded, and Sergt. Hiram Johnson is taking up the colors to bear them onward. It seems that the enemy is firing at the colors, for as the regiment is nearing Willoughby Run—see! Hiram Johnson, too, is wounded, and John Stamper, of the color guards, has the Stars and Bars. Briers, reeds, and underbrush impede the advance of the regiment at Willoughby Run; and as the enemy's artillery (Cooper's Battery), on the hill to our right, gets an enfilade fire on the regiment thus entangled, our men are suffering a frightful loss. To the right of us and to the left of us men are falling, some killed, more wounded. Private Stamper, with the flag, falls just as he is entering the underbrush. G. W. Kelly, one of the color bearers, raises the fallen banner and moves onward. As he leaps to the farther bank of Willoughby Run, he misses his footing and falls prone on the bank. "Get up, George, and come on," says a comrade. "Can't, Lewis; I'm hit. I believe my leg is broken." "What hit you?" "Piece of shell. There it lies. Give it to me, please. I'm going to take it home for a souvenir. Take the flag, Lewis." And now L. A. Thomas, of Company F, has the colors. Scores of men are hit while the regiment is crossing the Run and getting into proper position on the other side.[107]

After this bloody crossing of the creek, the 26th North Carolina moved up the steep eastern bank and entered into a deadly close-combat struggle with the 24th Michigan and the 19th Indiana of the Iron Brigade. This legendary clash would be engraved into the pages of history because of the high casualty rate on both sides. In 1903 Lt. Col. Lane narrated the horrific tale:

The engagement was becoming desperate. It seemed as if the bullets were as thick as hailstones in a storm. At his post on the right of the regiment and ignorant as to what was taking place on the left, Lieut. Col. Lane hurries to the center. He is met by Col. Burgwyn, who informs him "it is all right in the center and on the left: we have broken the first line of the enemy." The reply comes, "We are in line on the right, Colonel." ...At this time the colors have been cut down ten times, the color guard all killed or wounded. We have now struck the second line of the enemy where the fighting is the fiercest and the killing the deadliest. Suddenly Capt. W.W. McCreery, assistant inspector general of the brigade, rushes forward and speaks to Col. Burgwyn. He bears him a message. "Tell him," says General Pettigrew, "this regiment has covered itself with glory today." Delivering these encouraging words, Capt. McCreery... seizes the fallen flag, waves it aloft and advancing to the front, is shot through the heart and falls, bathing the flag in his life's blood. Lieut. George Wilcox of Co. "H." now rushes forward and pulling the flag from under the dead hero, advances with it. In a few steps he also falls with two wounds in his body. The line hesitates; the crisis is reached; the colors must advance. The gallant Burgwyn leaps forward, takes them up and again the line moves forward.... At this juncture, a brave private, Franklin Honeycutt, of Union county, takes the colors and Burgwyn turns... Burgwyn delivers Pettigrew's message. At that instant he falls with a bullet through both lungs, and at the same moment brave Honeycutt falls dead only a few steps in advance ... [Lane] ... finds the colors still down. Col. Burgwyn and the brave Franklin Honeycutt lying by them. Now or never the regiment must advance. He raises the flag. Lieut. Blair of Company I, rushes out, saying: "No man can take those colors and live." Lane replies, "It is my time to take them now," and shouting at the top of his voice while advancing with the flag, says: "Twenty-sixth, follow me."[108]

Despite catastrophic casualties, the North Carolinians succeeded in pushing the Iron Brigade out of Herbst Woods. During this advance, Lt. Col. Lane was severely wounded. A member of the regiment summarized the sentiments of many of the men at this time: "The red field is won, but at what cost to victor, as well as to vanquished."[109]

Meanwhile, on Burgwyn's right the 11th North Carolina had crashed into the left flank of the 19th Indiana of the Iron Brigade. Lt. W.B. Taylor of Company A wrote: "we stood within 20 yards of each other for about 15 moments but they had to give way and when they [did] we just mowed them down...."[110] As the 19th Indiana's position was within yards of Willoughby's Run, much of this fighting took place on both sides of the creek, and many of the casualties were likely sustained on the Harmon farm. During the fighting, Maj. Egbert A. Ross, 11th North Carolina, was severely wounded by an artillery projectile. The young officer lived for just four hours afterward and was buried in the Springs Hotel Woods near where his

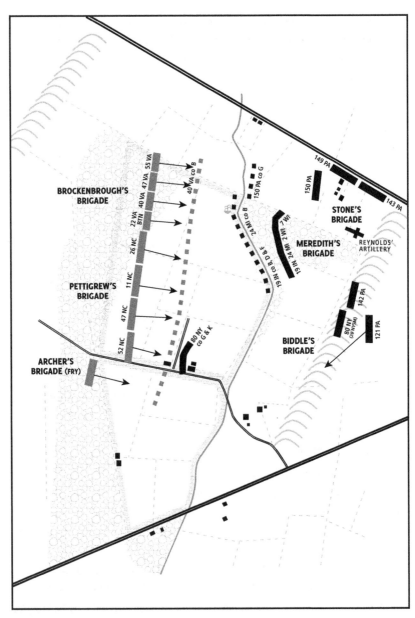

GEN. HENRY HETH'S ATTACK ACROSS THE HARMON FARM

regiment camped that night. Lt. Taylor "got a piece of plank and put his name on it with his rank for a head board."[111] Col. Collett Leventhorpe was also wounded during this costly engagement, leaving a captain in command of the regiment. After severe fighting, the 19th Indiana and 24th Michigan were forced back, along with the 2nd and 7th Wisconsin to their right. The Iron Brigade had been routed.[112]

On the right of Pettigrew's brigade, casualties were not particularly high during the first stages of the assault. One soldier wrote that it was "a grand spectacle" as Col. George H. Faribault's 47th North Carolina stepped out of the Springs Hotel Woods. While the 26th and 11th were partly concealed by Herbst Woods as they advanced, the 47th and 52nd were in plain view of Union artillerists on McPherson's Ridge. A member of the 47th remembered that the cannon fire created great gaps in the line. The low ground at Willoughby's Run provided brief cover for Faribault's Tar Heels, who then moved "up a hill through a wheat field," crashing into three of Col. Chapman Biddle's regiments. The struggle "grew hotter and hotter, men ... falling in every direction."[113] Eventually the 47th succeeded in pushing these units back toward the Seminary with help from the unit on its right, the 52nd North Carolina.

Meanwhile, Captains Baldwin and Cunningham of the 20th New York State Militia must have watched in awe and horror as the butternut line of the 52nd North Carolina slowly approached. Their position would soon be untenable. Amelia Harmon remembered listening intently from the basement of her home:

> Of a sudden there came a scurrying of quick feet, a loud clattering on the stairway above, a slamming of doors and then for an instant— silence! With a sickening dread we waited for the next act in the drama. A swish like the mowing of grass on the front lawn, then a dense shadow darkened the low grated cellar windows. It is the sound and the shadow of hundreds of marching feet. We can see them to the knees only but the uniforms are the Confederate gray! Now we understand the scurrying feet overhead. Our soldiers have been driven back, have retreated, left the house, and left us to our fate![114]

Col. James K. Marshall, a Virginia Military Institute graduate, led the 52nd North Carolina Infantry at Gettysburg. Descended from the prominent Marshall family of Virginia, he was a distant relative of Gen. Robert E. Lee. He survived the July 1 attack only to lose his life two days later during Longstreet's Assault.[115]

From the high ground on McPherson's Ridge, Capt. John Cook of the 20th New York State Militia witnessed the intimidating Confederate advance:

> ...from the forest in front appeared a long brown line of the enemy's infantry. In poetry and romance the Confederate uniform is gray. In

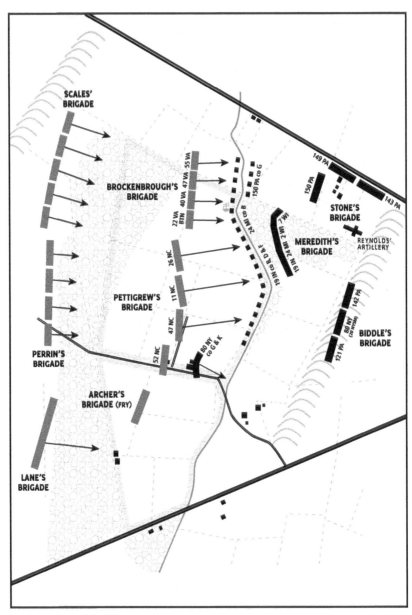

SCALES' BRIGADE

BROCKENBROUGH'S BRIGADE

55 VA

47 VA

40 VA

22 VA BTN

26 NC

11 NC

47 NC

52 NC

PETTIGREW'S BRIGADE

PERRIN'S BRIGADE

ARCHER'S BRIGADE (FRY)

LANE'S BRIGADE

150 PA Co G

24 NY Co B

19 IN Co B, D & F

80 NY Co G & K

19 IN 24 MI 2 WI 7 WI

MEREDITH'S BRIGADE

REYNOLDS' ARTILLERY

149 PA

150 PA

143 PA

STONE'S BRIGADE

142 PA

86 NY (20 NYSM)

121 PA

BIDDLE'S BRIGADE

HETH'S ATTACK AND WITHDRAWAL OF UNION INFANTRY FROM THE HARMON HOUSE

actual service it was a butternut brown, and on those fellows who faced us at short range was, owing to their long campaign, as dirty, disreputable, and unromantic as can well be imagined.[116]

Capt. J. Frank Sterling of the 121st Pennsylvania also recalled the Confederate attack in a letter written shortly after the battle: "It was indeed a beautiful sight to see the rebels advancing from the woods in line of battle with their flags flying as they marched steadily on...."[117]

As the 52nd North Carolina approached the Harmon farmhouse and barn, Companies K and G of the 20th New York State Militia stubbornly held their ground, doing "fearful execution upon the advancing enemy, without being themselves exposed."[118] But the situation soon became desperate when Marshall's troops—likely from Company E of the 52nd North Carolina, commanded by Capt. Benjamin F. Little—surrounded the buildings on three sides and began setting fire to some of the out-houses.[119]

At this critical moment, the New Yorkers withdrew from the Harmon house. "Moving through a ravine southerly and covered in a measure by a small party of cavalry, they made good their escape and rejoined the regiment that evening on Cemetery Hill."[120] The supporting cavalrymen—probably from the 8th Illinois—also helped to delay the main line of the 52nd North Carolina's advance toward Willoughby's Run.

After the Federal skirmishers had withdrawn, Col. Marshall was determined to prevent further enemy use of the Harmon farm structures. He immediately ordered his men to burn the house and barn. Capt. Benjamin F. Little, Company E, recalled: "The McLean [Harmon] House was burned by order of Col. Marshall because of the sharpshooters firing upon us. The men burned it very reluctantly, but it was the only way we could get them out. We had no artillery. Burnt it as we were making the advance."[121]

As some of Marshall's men rushed into the house, they were confronted by Amelia Harmon and her aunt, Rachel Finefrock. Amelia remembered:

> We rushed up the cellar steps to the kitchen. The barn was in flames and cast a lurid glare through the window. The house was filled with Rebels and they were deliberately firing it. They had taken down a file of newspapers for kindling, piled on books, rugs and furniture, applied matches to ignite the pile, and already a tiny flame was curling upward. We both jumped on the fire in the hope of extinguishing it, and plead with them in pity to spare our home. But there was no pity in those determined faces. They proceeded to carry

out their full purpose and told us to get out or we would burn with it. They were the "Louisiana Tigers," they boasted, and tigers indeed they were.[122]

A slightly different account of the confrontation appeared in the *Adams Sentinel* on December 8, 1863:

On the repulse of the Union cavalry the rebels announced their intention of firing the building, in accordance with the laws of war; it having been used (they said) as a fort. The family, and the young lady protested, explaining that the occupation was forcible, and not with their consent, the young lady adding that her mother, who was not now living, was a Southern woman, and that she would blush for her parentage if Southern men could thus fire the house of defenseless females, and turn them out in the midst of a battle. One of the ruffians then approached her and proposed, in a confidential manner, that if she would prove that she was not a renegade Southerner by hurrahing for the Southern Confederacy, he would see what could be done. The young heroine indignantly refused, and abandoning her burning house with her aunt, ran the gauntlet of the fire of two armies.[123]

This article omits an intriguing detail that Amelia Harmon mentioned in her 1915 account. Here she said that the "Louisiana Tigers" were responsible for burning her house. This is impossible as there were no Louisiana soldiers near the Harmon farm on July 1.[124] Amelia may have added this detail because her mother, Amelia Jewell Camp, had lived in Louisiana before Amelia was born. She may have fabricated this small piece of the story to create irony. It is also possible that soldiers of the 52nd North Carolina claimed to be "Louisiana Tigers" in order to shift the blame to a much more infamous group of rebels.[125]

In any event, the blaze was witnessed by many spectators around the battlefield. The "magnificent house and barn, with all the out-buildings, were soon a roaring mass of flames."[126] It is unclear whether the two-story smoke/washhouse was burned. It appears on post-battle maps, while the house and barn are merely outlined.[127] *New-York Herald* reporter G. W. Hosmer wrote:

...a party of about one hundred rebels stole through the woods well up on Doubleday's left flank, and fired a large barn, one of those immense magazines of breadstuffs that in Pennsylvania so overpeer the comparatively small farmhouses. An immense black column of smoke soon began to ascend from the roof thereof, breaking out presently into a white, sulphurous cloud, and then into a fierce red blaze. Under cover of this fire the rebel skirmishers exchanged numerous shots with a line of skirmishers from the cavalry on our extreme left.[128]

Because we know that Union cavalry was covering the retreat of Baldwin and Cunningham when they withdrew from the Harmon farm, Hosmer may have witnessed the covering fire directed by the 8th Illinois at elements of the 52nd North Carolina who were in the process of burning the Harmon barn and house. It is also possible that Hosmer was referring to the John Herbst barn, which was burned shortly after Harmon's structures were put to the torch.[129]

The burning of the Harmon farm was mentioned in several post-battle writings, including Andrew B. Cross's *Battle of Gettysburg and the Christian Commission* and Edward Everett's well-known oration delivered at the dedication of the Soldier's National Cemetery in Gettysburg. Another unique account of the Harmon farm came from historian John Bachelder:

> The buildings were occupied by a detachment from the 20th New York State Militia. Shots were exchanged, and a sharp fusillade kept up. It is reported that when the final charge was made, and these buildings were passed, the chaplain of the 52nd North Carolina regiment, believing in his enthusiasm that the confederate cause required it, applied the torch, notwithstanding the earnest remonstrations of the old man and his daughter in charge.[130]

Bachelder's passage raises several questions. According to a member of the 26th North Carolina, the chaplains of Pettigrew's brigade were reportedly absent on July 1. In adddition, Capt. Benjamin F. Little of the 52nd North Carolina clearly stated that Col. James K. Marshall ordered the burning of the farm.[131] Finally, the "old man" to whom Bachelder refers is not mentioned in Amelia Harmon's detailed account; she mentions only her aunt.

As Amelia and Rachel left their burning home, men of the 52nd North Carolina crossed Willoughby's Run. During this advance, the 8th Illinois Cavalry continued to torment them. Company B of the 52nd, commanded by Lt. W.E. Kyle, was deployed to combat the stubborn troopers. "This gallant officer succeeded in holding the cavalry in check and finally drove them from our flank." According to one account, Col. Marshall was forced to deploy the regiment in square formation because of this heavy fire.

Despite these obstacles, the 52nd North Carolina continued its advance across the Herbst farm, crashing into the left flank of the 121st Pennsylvania of Col. Chapman

Biddle's brigade. In the ensuing fight "the gallant Captain McCain, of Company I, fell dead, pierced by a Minie ball, while leading his company in the thickest of the fight." At another part of the line, "the young and chivalrous Captain Blackburn, of Company K, fell dead at the head of his company while leading his men to victory."[132]

To Pettigrew's right, Fry's (formerly Archer's) brigade had encountered its own problems. Before the attack the brigade was positioned somewhere between the Mill Road and the Fairfield Road. Its regiments may have been aligned in the following order from left to right: 7th Tennessee, 14th Tennessee, 5th Alabama Battalion, 13th Alabama, 1st Tennessee.[133] When the attack commenced, men of the brigade noticed the 8th Illinois Cavalrymen along the Fairfield Road. Col. Fry quickly shifted his men south to prevent a flank attack and thus Archer's brigade did not move very far from the Springs Hotel Woods during the advance. However, the fields of the Stallsmith farm were not a particularly safe position as artillery shells were constantly exploding in the vicinity.[134]

Help was on the way for the battered men of Heth's division. Behind them, Maj. Gen. William Dorsey Pender's fresh division was already in motion. On the right of the line was Brig. Gen. James Henry Lane's North Carolina brigade. Its regiments were in line, from left to right: 33rd North Carolina, 18th North Carolina, 28th North Carolina, 37th North Carolina, 7th North Carolina.[135] (It was the men of Lane's brigade who had mortally wounded Confederate Gen. "Stonewall" Jackson at Chancellorsville just months before. Ironically, during their march across the Harmon farm, Lane's North Carolinians passed the smoldering remains of the "McLean Mansion," former home of Jackson's distant relatives.)

During the midday lull, Gen. Lane had ordered "the Seventh Regiment to deploy as a strong line of skirmishers" on the right of the brigade and "at right angles" to the main line.[136] He also placed the regiment in this position to protect the brigade's flank, which was already being harassed by the 8th Illinois Cavalry. Later in the afternoon these men were brought forward to Heth's assistance. Lane wrote:

> ...we gained ground to the right, and on emerging from the woods in which Pettigrew's brigade had been formed, I found that my line had passed Archer's, and that my entire front was unmasked.[137]

Maj. Beveridge of the 8th Illinois Cavalry recalled that his regiment was ordered to withdraw at about the same time that Lane was exiting the woods. Beveridge then moved the regiment toward McPherson's Ridge. However, he did not have time to order in the one squadron that was on picket farther out on the Fairfield Road. These men were cut off by Lane's advance.[138]

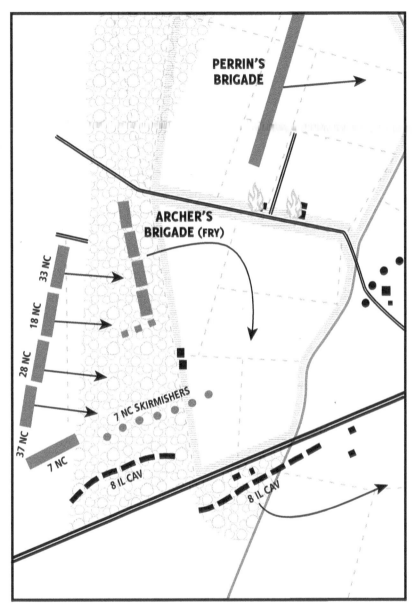

PERRIN'S BRIGADE

ARCHER'S BRIGADE (FRY)

33 NC

18 NC

28 NC

37 NC

7 NC

7 NC SKIRMISHERS

8 IL CAV

8 IL CAV

THE AFTERNOON ADVANCES OF LANE AND FRY ACROSS THE STALLSMITH FARM

Lt. Marcellus Jones recalled that the abandoned squadron received the order to retreat but chose instead to attack the right flank of Lane's brigade.

GEN. JAMES H. LANE (USAMHI)

> The squadron on picket had not come in. At the time they received the order of recall, they discovered the advance of Pender's division and they were hurrying upon his right flank. Pender's division emerged from the woods in echelon, from left to right. The right coming out of the woods near the position vacated by us. The squadron on picket appeared in the orchard to the left of the Fairfield road and opened fire. Pender's whole division halted. His right brigade changed front and fired a volley.[139]

It is unlikely that Pender's entire division was halted by the squadron's fire. However, Lane's brigade was considerably delayed by the Illinois troopers. The 7th North Carolina was even forced to break away from the brigade "on account of the threatening attitude of the cavalry."[140]

Now separated from Perrin's brigade, the majority of Lane's North Carolinians continued forward cautiously, crossing Willoughby's Run near the Herbst house. They pressed on across the Fairfield Road where they engaged other units of Gamble's brigade in Shultz Woods on Seminary Ridge. Due to delaying actions by the 8th Illinois Cavalry, Pender's attacking force had been greatly reduced.

Earlier that day, Abner Perrin's rebel brigade had deployed on Herr's Ridge. These four South Carolina regiments were likely arranged in the following left-to-right order: 14th South Carolina, 1st South Carolina, 12th South Carolina, 13th South Carolina.[141]

When the order to advance reached Perrin's brigade, every man rose to his feet. Rufus Harling of the 14th South Carolina wrote: "At the word 'Attention' we formed in [an] open field, in plain view of the enemy. The orders were, 'hold your fire men, and close in with the enemy.' We advanced in splendid order...."[142]

Perrin's brigade quickly moved through the Springs Hotel Woods and emerged in an open meadow on the Harmon farm.[143] During this advance they were harassed by Union artillery fire. James F.J. Caldwell of the 1st South Carolina (Provisional Army) recalled:

> Heth's division, which was on the first line, became regularly engaged. Volleys of musketry ran along his lines, accompanied with

the shrill rebel cheer. Many of the enemy's balls fell among us, who were on the second line, but I recall no farther [sic] result than the startling of our nerves by their whistling past our ears and slapping the trees before us....[144]

Berry Benson of the 1st South Carolina belonged to a detachment of sharpshooters assigned to guard the right flank of the line. These men marched out toward the Fairfield Road to hold back the 8th Illinois Cavalry. After arriving near the road, Benson was ordered to deliver a note to Gen. Pender and so immediately moved toward McPherson's Ridge from the direction of the Fairfield Road. As he approached the Harmon farm, something caught his attention: "I could see some large houses on fire. Inquiring my way, I found it led past them, in fact, between two of them. I went on, passing numbers of wounded men and dead horses, and presently came to Pettigrew's Brigade."[145]

As Perrin's men neared Willoughby's Run, Amelia Harmon and Rachel Finefrock had just left the burning house. Rushing to safety, they were noticed by many soldiers of Perrin's brigade, including a member of the 13th South Carolina who remembered seeing some "greatly distressed" women who had been driven from their home.[146] Amelia remembered this terrible time:

> We fled from our burning home only to encounter worse horrors. The first Rebel line of battle had passed the house and were now engaged in a hot skirmish in the gorge of Willoughby's Run. The second was just abreast of the barn, and at that moment were being hotly attacked by the Union troops with shot and shell! We were between the lines! To go toward town would be to walk into the jaws of death. Only one way was open—through the ranks of the whole Confederate army to safety in its rear! Bullets whistled past our ears, shell burst and scattered their deadly contents all about us. On we hurried—wounded men falling all around us, the line moving forward as they fired it seemed with deadly precision, past what seemed miles of artillery with horses galloping like mad toward the town. We were objects of wonder and amazement that was certain, but few took time to listen to our story, and none believed it. All kept hurrying us to the rear. "Go on, go on," they shouted, "out of reach of the grape and canister!"[147]

Meanwhile, Perrin's brigade continued to advance toward Willoughby's Run. Col. Joseph N. Brown, 14th South Carolina, wrote: "passing a burning house on our right and crossing a small run, the brigade mounted the hill beyond and passed over

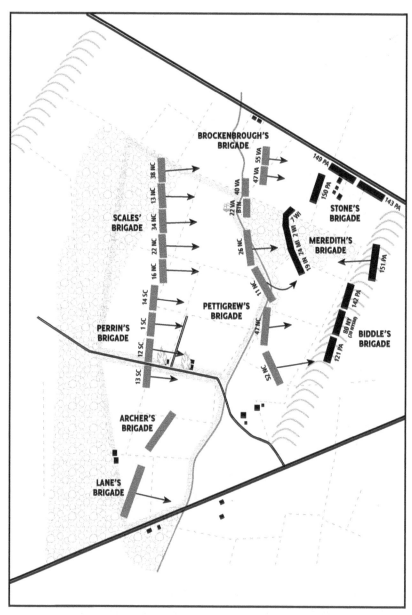

THE AFTERNOON ATTACKS OF HETH AND PENDER

the crippled lines of Gen. Pettigrew's brigade...."[148]

By this time many wounded North Carolinians of Pettigrew's brigade had retreated to the ravine of Willoughby's Run where they enjoyed relative safety. As Perrin's men reached this area, they could see Chapman Biddle's brigade withdrawing from McPherson's Ridge. The field of advance was now open from the creek to the Lutheran Theological Seminary.[149]

Before moving onto the Herbst farm, Perrin halted his brigade at Willoughby's Run. Here he cautioned his men to hold their fire until within range of the enemy. Soon after, the South Carolinians continued forward past Pettigrew's weary lines and pushed forward toward Seminary Ridge, where a desperate fight ensued.[150]

Brig. Gen. Alfred M. Scales's brigade formed the left flank of Pender's line. Earlier in the day Scales's men had reached Herr's Ridge on the south side of the Chambersburg Pike. According to historian John Bachelder, the regiments of the brigade were positioned, from left to right: 38th North Carolina, 13th North Carolina, 34th North Carolina, 22nd North Carolina, 16th North Carolina.[151]

During the climactic afternoon attack, Scales's brigade advanced down the eastern slope of Herr's Ridge, across both the Harmon farm and the neighboring Abraham Spangler farm. On this open ground, Scales's men were conspicuous targets for Union artillery, which did great damage to the Tar Heels. As they approached Willoughby's Run, the men passed over Brockenbrough's Virginians, who were apparently out of ammunition. The brigade then ascended the slope of McPherson's Ridge and helped to dislodge Col. Roy Stone's Bucktails. Scales pressed forward toward the Lutheran Seminary and, with Perrin and Lane on his right, helped to collapse the Union line on Seminary Ridge. During the attack the brigade endured murderous artillery fire that crippled the North Carolina regiments in the fields west of the Seminary, and Scales was severely wounded during the struggle. After a severe clash on Seminary Ridge, Pender had succeeded in removing the Federals from their last position on the west side of Gettysburg.[152]

When the smoke cleared, thousands of Union and Confederate soldiers, dead and maimed, lined the fields and woodlots from Herr's Ridge to Seminary Ridge. Among them lay the severely wounded Col. Henry K. Burgwyn, Jr., 26th North Carolina. Eventually, two soldiers reached his nearly lifeless body and began to carry him to the rear using a blanket for support. Burgwyn was alert enough to ask William M. Cheek, a member of his regiment, to help, and together the three North Carolinians carried their colonel back across

GEN. ALFRED SCALES (LOC)

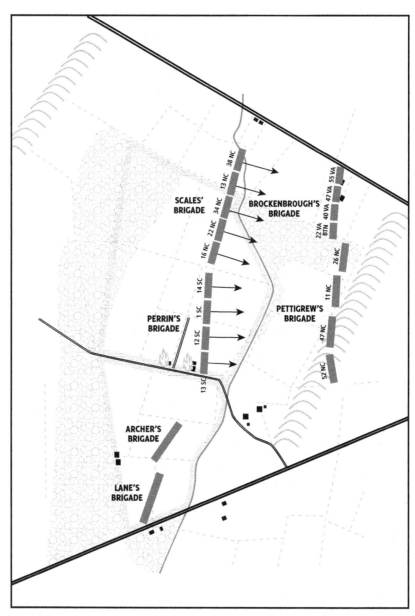

PENDER COMES TO HETH'S AID

Willoughby's Run onto the Harmon farm. "We carried him some distance towards the place where our line of battle had been formed." At some point a South Carolina lieutenant approached the soldiers and helped them by taking hold of a portion of the blanket. A member of this group remembered:

> Col. Burgwyn did not seem to suffer much, but asked the lieutenant to pour some water on his wound. He was put down upon the ground while the water was poured from canteens upon him. His coat was taken off and I stooped to take his watch, which was held around his neck by a silk cord. As I did so the South Carolina lieutenant seized the watch, broke the cord, put the watch in his pocket and started off with it. I demanded the watch, telling the officer that he should not thus take away the watch of my colonel and that I would kill him as sure as powder would burn, with these words cocking my rifle and taking aim. I made him come back and give up the watch, at the same time telling him he was nothing but a thief, and then ordering him to leave, which he did.[153]

It is impossible to determine exactly where this incident took place, but it is likely that it was on the Harmon farm. Although possibly exaggerated, the preceding account reflects the bitterness that existed between soldiers from different states. Cheek continued:

> Colonel Burgwyn said to me that he would never forget me, and I shall never forget the look he gave me as he spoke these words. We then picked him up again and carried him very close to the place where we had formed in line of battle. Captain Young, of General Pettigrew's staff, came up and expressed much sympathy with Colonel Burgwyn. The latter said that he was very grateful for the sympathy, and added, "The Lord's will be done. We have gained the greatest victory in the war. I have no regret at my approaching death. I fell in the defense of my country." About that time a shell exploded very near us and took off the entire top of the hat of captain Brewer, who had joined our party. I left and went to search for one of our litters...as the bearers and myself came up to the spot where Colonel Burgwyn was lying on the ground, we found that he was dying. I sat down and took his hand in my lap. He had very little to say, but I remember that his last words were that he was entirely satisfied with everything, and "The Lord's will be done." Thus he died, very quietly and resigned. I never saw a braver man than he. He was always cool under fire and knew

exactly what to do, and his men were devoted to him.[154]

Young Col. Burgwyn may have died beneath the canopy of the Springs Hotel Woods. It is also possible that he died on Herr's Ridge, which was where his regiment was first positioned upon its arrival that morning. Burgwyn was temporarily buried on Charles B. Polly's farm north of the Chambersburg Pike, next to Capt. Campbell T. Iredell of the 47th North Carolina and Capt. William Wilson of the 26th North Carolina.[155] Burgwyn was remembered as "tall, strong, handsome, and unusually commanding in appearance for one so young.... Both in mind and character he was mature."[156]

As Henry Burgwyn succumbed to his wounds, Amelia Harmon and Rachel Finefrock continued their journey west toward safety. Amelia recalled:

> At last, after we had walked perhaps two miles, we came upon a group
> of officers and newspaper men in conference under a tree. We told
> them our story. The officers looked incredulous, the newspaper men
> attentive. One of these, the Confederate correspondent of the "London
> Times," seemed greatly interested in our tale, and was, I believe, the
> only one who credited it fully. He courteously offered to conduct us
> to a place of safety still farther to the rear. Dismounting he walked
> with us, showing great sympathy, and assuring us that the ruffians
> who had fired our house would meet with condign punishment at the
> hands of Gen. Lee. Also that we would be fully reimbursed by him
> for our property. (In Confederate money of course). He placed us in
> an empty cottage, and went directly to Gen. Lee's headquarters, then
> quite close by. He returned shortly saying he had seen Lee in person,
> told him our story, and he had promised to station a guard around
> the house while the battle lasted, and send us rations every day.[157]

The newspaperman that Amelia mentioned was probably Francis Charles Lawley, a correspondent for *The Times*, a London newspaper. Although Amelia indicated that Lawley published her story, historians have been unable to find such an account.[158]

Meanwhile, the four brigades of Heth's division returned to the Springs Hotel Woods to rest and recuperate. Many of these units likely camped on the Harmon farm. Lt. Col. Shepard, 7th Tennessee, described the position of Archer's brigade (now commanded by Col. Fry): "...we lay in position upon a road upon the right of our line."[159] It is unclear whether Shepard was referring to the Fairfield Road or the Mill Road. Given the brigade's position during the afternoon of July 1, along the Fairfield Road is more logical. A member of the 55th North Carolina also indicated in a post-battle reminiscence that his brigade had camped in the Springs Hotel Woods: "[Davis's Brigade] was moved from its position on the railroad cut near the

Seminary to a piece of woods across Willoughby Run, west of the mineral springs, and there rested during the 2d."[160]

Confederates of Heth's division were not the only soldiers to occupy the Harmon farm on the evening of July 1. A group of prisoners, primarily from John C. Robinson's division of the Union First Corps, was also sent there. Samuel G. Boone, 88th Pennsylvania, wrote: "We were moved...to a point on Willoughby Run, now known as the Katalysine Spring, where we remained until the commencement of the retreat on July 4."[161]

Located near the northeast corner of the Harmon farm, this spring was likely used by Confederates of Heth's division who were camped nearby. In his 1873 tourist guide, historian John Bachelder wrote about the use of the spring during the battle:

> The Katalysine Spring, now so widely sought, then gushed unknown from the earth, placidly meandering their course, as the wild thunders of the fierce struggle shook the very heavens, and their sweet and peaceful waters assuaged the fiery thirst, alike, of the men in blue and the men in gray.[162]

Another unique account relating to the Katalysine Spring appeared in an 1890s Springs Hotel brochure:

> The Confederates, who obtained possession of the Spring after the first day's battle, used it for drinking and culinary purposes, and mistook its occasional eccentric therapeutical action for the operation of poison, which they supposed had been mixed with its waters; but soon discovered their mistake, on learning from some of the residents the tradition which attached to the Spring.[163]

Although this account is intriguing, no factual evidence supports it. It is unlikely that any Confederate soldier made such a claim. If such a record exists, it has yet to be discovered by the author.

On July 2, Gen. James Longstreet's corps arrived on the field. After reaching an elevated area near the Black Horse Tavern, Longstreet's men came in view of Little Round Top. After conversing with his generals, Longstreet chose to march back toward the Herr Tavern and select a different route in order to remain hidden from the enemy's view. This movement has become widely known as the "Circuitous March." It is difficult to know the exact route that Longstreet's divisions took to reach Seminary Ridge, but they may well have crossed both the Harmon and Stallsmith farms.[164] Capt. O.H. Miller of Georgia wrote that his regiment "marched to the right, on the west side of the branch and east of the McLean House."[165] If the captain was indeed referring to the Harmon house (formerly the Charles McLean house), this would indicate that some of Longstreet's men marched across the Harmon farm. John Bachelder suggested that part of Richard Anderson's division of Hill's corps used a small farm lane that connected the Mill Road with the Fairfield Road. This lane was located just west of the Stallsmith farm buildings.[166]

During the night of July 2, Heth's division was ordered to the Confederate front, vacating the Springs Hotel Woods for the last time. Meanwhile, somewhere west of Herr's Ridge, Amelia Harmon and Rachel Finefrock were housed in an abandoned cottage. Years later Amelia wrote:

> The guard soon appeared and patrolled around the house day and night during those three terrible days. Every day our rations of bread, bacon and coffee were furnished, and the guard were most respectful. But they were awful days of suspense and dread for we could hear the raging of the battle three miles away on the Round Tops, and our nights were filled with horror.[167]

The final division of Longstreet's corps, that of Gen. George E. Pickett, arrived on the morning of July 3. Historian Kathleen Georg Harrison believes that these men also used the lane between the Mill Road and the Fairfield Road to reach their designated position on Seminary Ridge.

Later that day the men would take part in "Pickett's Charge," one of the most famous infantry assaults in American history.[168]

Aftermath

Destruction of the Harmon Farm

After the overwhelming defeat of "Pickett's Charge" on July 3, Gen. Lee's army began its retreat, moving southwest along the Fairfield Road toward Maryland and, eventually, the Shenandoah Valley. Of the battle's aftermath Amelia Harmon wrote:

> On the fourth morning we found that our guard had silently vanished away, and going out to reconnoiter we saw the last of Lee's wagon train disappearing over the hills. There was no breakfast that morning nor did we have any until late afternoon, when we reached an inhabited house which proved to be that of the then editor of the "Gettysburg Compiler." Here we received a cordial welcome, and were urged to remain over night when it would be safer to go "home."[169]

At the same time, Union troops crept cautiously through the streets of Gettysburg. Amelia Harmon recalled her journey back to the Harmon farm the following day:

> This was not until the following afternoon when we footed the distance across the fields, for there was not a horse or vehicle to be found in all the country. I will not describe the sickening sights of the ground over which we passed. I would that I myself could forget them. When we reached the site of our home, a prosperous farm house five days before, there appeared only a blackened ruin and the silence of death. The chapter is closed. Here I draw the curtain and allow the scene to fade into the shadow of the past.[170]

It is unclear where the Harmons lived directly after the Battle of Gettysburg. Certainly the "McLean Mansion" was not immediately rebuilt. A list of structures destroyed during the battle published by the *Adams Sentinel* on July 14 included the Harmon house and barn.[171]

Early Gettysburg post-battle maps help to clarify the condition of the buildings. Two of the earliest maps were drawn by John Bachelder and S. G. Elliot in 1863–64. Bachelder's map shows the Harmon structures on fire, with a large orchard and a line representing the 20th New York State Militia's position at the house. Elliot's burial map indicates that both the barn and house were destroyed, but the smoke/washhouse appears to be intact. It is plausible that the brick exterior of the house was not entirely destroyed and thus appeared to Amelia Harmon as a "blackened ruin."[172]

After the war David Finefrock and William Comfort both filed claims for damages to their property. From these documents we know that there were ten acres of wheat, five acres of rye, and a potato patch on the property at the time of the battle. We also know that there were at least five sheep and eleven cattle on the farm, all of which were stolen or killed. Items from the house that were lost in the fire included a set of false teeth and an electromagnetic battery.[173]

A SMALL SECTION OF JOHN B. BACHELDER'S 1863 ISOMETRIC MAP SHOWING THE HARMON AND STALLSMITH FARMS (LOC)

Several post-battle writings refer to the condition of the Harmon house and surrounding area. In December of 1863, the "ruins" of the Harmon farm were still "visible from Seminary Ridge."[174] Two years later, a Gettysburg newspaper published an article that described the site: "…visible in the distance [are] the ruins of the M'Clean mansion and outhouses, which tell a tale in connection with the great battle."[175] In the early 1870s John Bachelder published an early battlefield tourist guide in which he wrote: "Having forded Willoughby Run we climb a hill, on which once stood the finest country residence in Adams County. Of this nothing now remains but blackened ruins, a sad reminder of the terrible ravages of war."[176]

A VIEW OF THE RECONSTRUCTED HARMON HOUSE TAKEN FROM THE OBSERVATORY OF THE SPRINGS HOTEL (GNMP)

The Harmon house was reconstructed in the 1880s or 1890s and eventually dismantled before the Country Club purchased the land in 1947. A 1900 article from the *Gettysburg Compiler* noted that "with some of the brick gathered from the ruins of the original buildings a small house, still standing, was afterwards constructed."[177] Today, the site of the Harmon house and barn is private property; modern houses have been constructed upon it.

Confederate Burials

During the Battle of Gettysburg, scores of Confederates perished on the fields of the Harmon farm. S. G. Elliot's 1864 burial map confirms this, showing sizable Confederate burial trenches just west of Willoughby's Run. Since it is unlikely that soldiers were carried across the creek for burial, they were probably killed in action west of the stream.[178] Dr. J. W. C. O'Neal, who documented many graves around the battlefield, located three 11th North Carolina burials along the creek. These were the graves of Lt. Edward Averett Rhodes and Lt. Thomas Watson Cooper of Company C, and Lt. James B. Lowrie of Company H. O'Neal recordeded another grave that was "in [the] field" west of Lt. Rhodes's grave. This was likely the resting place of Pvt. Alfred B. Howard, Company E, 26th North Carolina.[179] During the afternoon attack on July 1, this area was occupied by the 11th and 26th North Carolina regiments.

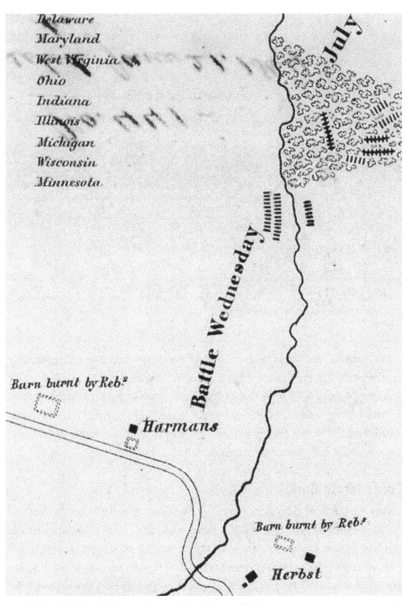

PART OF THE ELLIOT BURIAL MAP THAT INCLUDES THE HARMON FARM (LOC)

MAJ. EGBERT A. ROSS (HSRBNC)

An interesting story relating to 11th North Carolina casualties appears in the post-battle writings of Charles D. Walker. During the fighting, Lt. Rhodes of that regiment had apparently "seized the colors, and was in the act of advancing, cheering the men, when he was struck in the head by a Minie-ball, and fell, murmuring, 'Uh, God!' into the arms of his captain. His two young friends, Cooper and Lowrie, fell nearly at the same moment, and were buried that night by the officers on the spot where they fell...."

Col. Leventhorpe, commander of the regiment, sent a letter to the mother of young Rhodes in which he mentioned seeing the lieutenant shortly before his death: "Just as we were nearing the enemy...he remarked to me, with a smile 'we are marching in excellent line.'" At the time of first burial, the graves were apparently marked by a mere "barrel-stave" with the soldiers' names on it.[180] These men were later exhumed by their families and reinterred in North Carolina.

Another grave was specifically labeled on Elliot's map as "W.C. Co." This was located on the Abraham Spangler farm, just yards from the northern edge of the Harmon property. O'Neal noted in 1866 while passing by this grave: "Back of Gate House, near Vitchy [sic] Springs W.C.G." At that time, the spring on the Harmon farm was often compared to the famous Vichy Springs of France. This soldier may have been 32-year-old William Carter Gardner, a private in Company C, 55th Virginia, who was killed on July 1. Another soldier of the 55th Virginia, referred to simply as "J.J.G.," was buried west of Willoughby's Run on or near the Harmon farm. The marker indicated that he was also a member of Company E. This soldier was probably John J. Gouldman, who was killed on July 1. O'Neal wrote that the grave was located "North of Harman's [sic]...west of the Gatehouse." Perhaps the two Virginians were buried side by side.[181] On the south side of the Harmon farm, two Confederates of Company D, 52nd North Carolina, were temporarily buried. They were Pvt. James D. Leaman and Pvt. John H. Hancock. These graves were located in the Springs Hotel Woods beside the Mill Road.[182]

One day Dr. O'Neal came upon the grave of Maj. Egbert A. Ross, 11th North Carolina Infantry. Ross had been killed on July 1 and buried in the Springs Hotel Woods "South of Hares [Herr's] place." O'Neal also noted that Ross was removed from that location at some point.[183]

Reminders of the struggle that took place on the fields west of Gettysburg continued to be uncovered into the late nineteenth century. In October of 1877 a gruesome discovery was made on the Harmon farm:

> Calvin P. Culp was plowing on the Springs Hotel grounds, between the hotel and the lake, [when] he came across the remains of four Rebel bodies, supposed to have belonged to a North Carolina regiment, as the buttons bore the coat of arms of that state. One had been shot through the head, as shown by a bullet hole in the skull. The bones were gathered together, put into a box, and re-interred.[184]

These soldiers were probably members of the 26th or 11th North Carolina regiments of Pettigrew's brigade. It is unclear where the remains were reinterred; they may have been taken to the Springs Hotel Woods or across Willoughby's Run to Herbst Woods.

In 1890 remains were once again found on the Harmon farm near the Springs Hotel. While hunting on the property, Charles Lady unearthed a Confederate skeleton. Nearby were a felt hat and brass buttons, still intact decades after the fighting.[185]

The Harmon Family after the Battle

In 1865 Emanuel Harmon purchased the land south of the Mill Road from the heirs of Peter Stallsmith and reunited Reverend McLean's original 1819 tract.[186] At the time of the 1868–69 Warren Map survey, the old Stallsmith farm was labeled "D. Finnefrock" and consisted of two frame structures. This suggests that David and Rachel Finefrock had moved to one of these buildings. Because of the Warren Map, many current maps, books, and articles incorrectly identify the 1863 Stallsmith farm as belonging to David Finefrock.[187] In 1870 the Finefrock house was visited by a census taker. At that time the couple had one son, E. (short for Emanuel) Harmon Finefrock. This child was surely named after the elusive property owner who was almost certainly a relative. David W. Finefrock died in about 1880 at the age of 70 and is buried in Evergreen Cemetery.[188]

William Comfort does not appear in the 1870 census, but his wife, Mary (formerly Harmon), is listed as a domestic servant.

After the Civil War Amelia Harmon met George W. Miller of Gettysburg. They married in 1868 and raised four children, one of whom they named Jewell in honor of Amelia's mother. George was a prominent Methodist clergyman whose job required frequent moves in Pennsylvania, Delaware, Maryland, New York, and New Jersey. When George retired in 1910, the couple relocated to Asbury Park, New Jersey.[189]

In 1915, at nearly 70 years of age, Amelia summoned the strength to write an account of her experiences during the Battle of Gettysburg, which must have reawakened many frightful memories. Her account was published in the July 3, 1915, issue of the *Gettysburg Compiler.*

Evidently Amelia died soon thereafter. Her name has not been found in the 1920 census.

Part 2

Katalysine Springs

1865–69: A Rare and Valuable Mineral Spring

In 1865 Emanuel Harmon's fortunes changed. His Pennsylvania farm, virtually destroyed two years earlier, would soon become one of the most valuable properties in the region. On October 10, 1865, Professor Alfred M. Mayer of Pennsylvania (now Gettysburg) College conducted a chemical examination of the spring located on the Harmon farm and found its waters to be unique:

> On comparing it with other springs which have been subjected to analysis, I find that it approaches nearer to the celebrated Vichy waters than to any other.... The presence of the rare alkali Lithia in this spring, gives to it a scientific interest, and no doubt adds to its medicinal virtues.[190]

The name "Gettysburg Lithia Spring" was adopted, and shortly after Mayer's examination the spring was enlarged and its walls rebuilt. In addition to Lithia, many rich and supposedly "curative" minerals were found in the water: sodium, lithium, potassium, magnesium, iron, lime, sulphate of lime, chlorides, phosphates, and silica.[191] An article about the spring–"A National Watering Place"–published in the *Adams Sentinel* on November 21, 1865, included a staggering estimation of the spring's potential value:

> The intelligent and experienced spring-digger, who cleaned out and newly walled this spring the other day, estimated its capacity of discharging water at one hundred barrels per day. Reducing this estimate one half, and computing its value at twenty-five cents per pint...and we have the astounding sum total of ($3,300) three

thousand three hundred dollars per day, or, one million one hundred and four thousand dollars per annum.[192]

The article also included a poetic description of the Harmon farm:

> The spring is located in a quiet little vale, about midway between two groves some hundred yards from it, now denuded of their foliage, but which, when robed in their summer glories, must be exceedingly beautiful. One of these rises above it like the section of an amphitheater [Herbst Woods], and stretches away in the distance; the other forms the outer boundary of an intervening plain, into which the gentle elevation which form the miniature valley subside [the Springs Hotel Woods].[193]

In December of 1865, Emanuel Harmon sent a sample of the spring's water to Dr. Robert K. Stone, former personal physician to President Abraham Lincoln. Stone found that the water was "identical in some respects, and superior in others" to the famous Vichy water of France.[194] In a letter published the following week, Stone declared the spring to be among the "gaseous, alkaline, medicinal springs," although the water was "destitute of the taste, odor, or other signs by which such waters are invariably distinguished."[195]

As 1865 drew to a close, excitement was building throughout the area as word spread about the possibility of a resort hotel being built to accommodate future visitors to the spring and battlefield.

Emanuel Harmon's water was destined to become a household name. On January 6, 1866, news of his spring reached the national stage in Washington's *Daily National Republican*: "A new mineral spring has been discovered near Gettysburg, Pa., the water resembling that of Vichy."[196] Several weeks later a local paper updated the Gettysburg public about the spring's growing popularity and medical virtues:

> The mineral spring near this town still continues to attract the attention of our citizens, as well as of strangers. It has, as I am informed, proved efficient as a curative agent in quite a number of instances of rheumatic, kidney, and urinary diseases. It is now being used, I understand, by many persons of great respectability for various chronic complaints with fair prospects of success.[197]

In February and March of 1866, Gettysburg newspapers published several articles on the water that further compared it to the Vichy water of France. Interest in the water was building, and the elite of Gettysburg were ready to capitalize on it. On April 24 it was reported that the Gettysburg Lithia Springs Association had been formed with many prominent Gettysburgians as its members, including Legislator Edward McPherson and attorneys David McConaughy and David Wills.[198] On September 4 it was rumored that a bottling establishment would soon be built and that Gettysburg could become a "national watering place." Meanwhile, three new springs were discovered in close proximity to the original source. "These discoveries establish beyond a doubt the vast commercial value of this medicinal water."[199] On January 1, 1867, Governor John W. Geary, who had commanded a division at the Battle of Gettysburg, wrote a letter in support of the spring and its proponents.[200]

Despite this initial surge of fame, it appears that during the early months of 1867 plans did not move forward as quickly as the public had expected. However, the water was continually analyzed by respected scientists and physicians, and the spring was featured in a September 28, 1867, article in the *Medical and Surgical Reporter* written by Dr. John Bell. This exposure brought national attention to the property once again.[201] By October orders for the "Gettysburg Water" were arriving daily from New York, Philadelphia, and "western cities."[202]

On November 15 local papers reported that a "New York party" was negotiating with Emanuel Harmon for the right to bottle and sell the water. "These persons visited town last week, and have made a conditional purchase of property which they deemed important in the prosecution of their business."[203]

Emanuel Harmon's relationship with the New York company was tumultuous at best. After visiting the property, the businessmen gained the right to bottle the water, then began to purchase the surrounding land, probably intending to control passage to and from the spring. These actions may have contributed to their expulsion from the property by Harmon two years later.[204]

Around this time a photograph published by C.J. Tyson of Gettysburg—perhaps the first photograph recorded on the Harmon farm—showed a one-story wooden structure that had been constructed over the main source of the spring. The photograph's caption reads: "Lithia Springs, west of Gettysburg. Ground held by Rebels during the battle."[205]

Throughout the early months of 1868, "Gettysburg Water" was "extensively bottled, and shipped, to fill orders, to all parts of the country." The process was supervised by Doctor G.D. Smith, and large quantities of the water were sent by train to New York, "where the peculiarly valuable medicinal qualities of the water are extensively advertised."[206] About this time the name "Katalysine" was adopted for the water. Possibly of Greek origin, "Katalysine" may be a combination of words meaning "downward flowing" or, more pointedly, "laxative."[207] The earliest containers for the spring water were Saratoga-style bottles—thick glass, usually green, with the words "Gettysburg Katalysine Water" embossed in a circle.[208]

AN 1867 VIEW OF THE SPRINGHOUSE (FRASSANITO COLL.)

Meanwhile, the New York company that had been bottling Harmon's water continued to purchase large tracts of land around the spring. On January 8 newspapers announced that the capitalists had acquired the former Herr property west of the spring and also the Edward McPherson farm on the east side of Willoughby's Run. "The Company have leased the Springs from Mr. Harman, and by the above purchases control the grounds around them."[209]

The idea of an on-site resort once again grew popular during these early months of 1868. "It is probable that a number of cottages will ere long be put up, to be occupied by families and invalids attracted by the reputation of the water."[210] By June water sales reached an all-time high, and Dr. Smith was "pushing operations at the Gettysburg Katalysine Spring with all possible vigor." According to one article, about 250 dozen bottles were being shipped every day by the "large force of hands and improved machinery."[211]

In order to conduct business at the site, Dr. Smith created an "excellent road ... from the turnpike to the spring." This was apparently traveled so much that the toll gate near Willoughby's Run was moved closer to town in order to collect money from visitors to the spring. Smith also improved the property by adding shade trees, walking paths, grasses, and new fencing.[212] A June 1868 article described the new springhouse in detail: "The spring itself has been carefully walled up with heavy dressed granite, and enclosed in one end of the building used for bottling—the building itself being a neat and comfortable one, with piazza and office for accommodation of visitors."[213] Inside the building, the newspaperman witnessed Katalysine Spring employees at work:

> Everything, from the unpacking of empty bottles to the final packing and labeling of boxes is done in the building—washing empty bottles, filling with the Katalysine water, corking, labeling, wrapping, packing...employing about 30 hands. The whole process is rapid and systematic, the bottles passing from hand to hand in the various processes, without confusion. The corking is done very rapidly by air of ingenious machinery, and it is impossible to withdraw the cork without breaking or defacing, thus guarding against tampering with the water after leaving the establishment. Most of the employees are young girls, who receive good wages.... Teams are passing to and fro, bringing cases of empty bottles from the depot, and returning with cases of water bottled for the market...visitors to the Spring are always courteously received, and permitted to drink freely of the water without charge.[214]

Later that year the New York company added John Burns's property on Seminary Ridge to their growing list of acquisitions.[215] Tired of shipping the water "to every part of the country," Gettysburgians wanted to benefit more directly from the spring's popularity. The time was right for "a large Summer Hotel or a number of them" to be constructed near the spring. In August 1868 the unrealized Gettysburg Springs Hotel Project was revived.[216] By September it was gaining momentum, and on September 11 it was announced that Emanuel Harmon would give five acres of land near the spring on which the hotel could be built. At

AN 1860S KATALYSINE BOTTLE (AIDC)

A VIEW OF THE HARMON FARM, TAKEN FROM THE CUPOLA OF THE LUTHERAN SEMINARY, SHOWING PART OF THE HORSE RAILWAY AND SPRINGS HOTEL COMPLEX (GNMP)

the same time, investors began a drive to raise $30,000 for its construction.[217] To accommodate tourists and visitors, a new mode of transportation to and from the Harmon farm was proposed. A Horse Railway would be installed to connect the Gettysburg Train Station with the already bustling spring and the planned hotel. On October 16 a local newspaper reported:

> Work on the Horse Railway between town and the Katalysine Spring has been commenced in earnest. A large force of hands is employed on the grading, whilst another is engaged in getting out and delivering the cross-ties. The Railway has been laid down in a broad avenue, which will doubtless become one of the handsomest thoroughfares in the country.[218]

A portion of the railroad path is still used today as Springs Avenue, a Victorian-era neighborhood at the west end of Gettysburg Borough.

During October of 1868, construction of the railway progressed from town to the spring, crossing the campus of the Lutheran Seminary and cutting through the 1863 John Herbst farm:

JOHN B. BACHELDER, DEL.

GETTYSBURG SPRINGS HOTEL

KATALYSINE SPRING

BACHELDER'S ILLUSTRATION OF THE BRIDGE OVER WILLOUGHBY'S RUN WITH THE SPRINGS HOTEL IN THE DISTANCE (ACHS)

> The road will start at the Passenger Depot, run up Carlisle street to the Square, thence in a straight line to the foot of the Seminary grounds, where a slight curve to the south of the President's house will be made; thence direct to the Katalysine spring.[219]

At Willoughby's Run a bridge was built south of the spring "affording room for a railroad track and two carriage ways." Original bridge abutments are visible today along the creek.

Work continued on the railroad until December 4, when the project was suspended for the winter. The company formed to supervise the railroad was made up of both local and New York businessmen, with Gettysburgian Robert McCurdy serving as president.[220]

In late fall of 1868, a foundation was laid for the Springs Hotel, expected to accommodate up to 500 guests. If everything went according to plan, Emanuel Harmon's farm would become one of the most famous destinations in the country.[221]

1869: "Stroke of an Enchanter's Wand"

> Having some business on the Chambersburg Pike the other day, I deflected to the left at the gate-house and soon found myself in the little valley where bubbles "the Gettysburg Katalysine Spring." I was surprised to find that the silence and solitude which reigned here during the winter, had been superceded [*sic*] by bustle and activity, and by the sounds of merry voices, the tramping of many feet, the

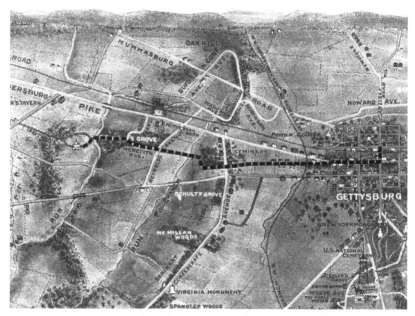

HORSE RAILWAY ROUTE BETWEEN GETTYSBURG TRAIN STATION AND SPRINGS HOTEL (LOC)

clanking of bottles and the creaking of machinery—in other words, that the bottling of this water for the spring trade had commenced. While reconnoitering the bottling operations, my attention was several times attracted by the passage of men and boys to and from the bottling establishment, and the south western portion of the glade, and turning my eyes in that direction I saw beyond the acclivity which intervened, the heads of a number of men moving about as if engaged in some occupation of more than ordinary interest. Being desirous of seeing whatever might be interesting in this now, important locality, I directed my steps thither, and came across the workmen employed upon a structure which had risen as if 'from the stroke of the enchanter's wand,' upon this, but a few years ago, wild and unfrequented spot.... The foundation walls of this building are constructed of red shale stone, but have not yet received their wooden superstructure.[222]

—March 19, 1869

The massive wooden hotel would be three stories high with an attic, the main section being "120 feet long and 44 feet deep" with a "wing extending back towards the south 80 x 38 feet" and would accommodate about 250 guests, fewer than originally estimated. The hotel was to be completed by June 20 in order to be ready for guests who would arrive in Gettysburg for the dedication of the Soldiers National Monument at the new National Cemetery.[223]

In March, as construction of the hotel moved forward, conflict erupted between Emanuel Harmon and the New York businessmen who were bottling Katalysine water. On March 30, 1869, Harmon terminated the company's lease and "ejected the employees of the company and placed his own agents in charge, at the same time posting up a notice." David W. Finefrock was likely one of Harmon's agents, as the 1870 census indicates this was his occupation. Harmon wrote:

> All agents of the Gettysburg Spring Company are forbidden to enter
> these premises or the grounds adjacent for the purpose of exercising
> authority or the powers of the lease thus abrogated, under penalties of
> trespass and of such summary expulsion as the laws justify.[224]

Somehow the New Yorkers had defaulted on their lease. Newspapers in Philadelphia and New York City also ran this story, noting that "the premises are still held by the employes of the owner during the day, and by watchmen during the night."[225]

It appears that the struggle over the spring nearly came to blows. On April 3, 1869, the *New York Times* included a story headlined "The Battle at Gettysburg."

> Latest news from "the front" proclaims a lull in the hostilities at
> Gettysburg. The other day, there were dread war-rumors from the
> historic battle-field. The proprietor of the Katalysyne [*sic*] Springs
> had "forcibly expelled" the lessees, a party of men was in charge of
> "the bottling establishment," and an "armed force was on duty to
> guard the Springs during the night." It was further reported that the
> enemy was "also mustering forces to regain possession, threatening
> serious consequences." Thus history was about to "repeat itself,"
> and...so the great battle of Gettysburg was likely to be duplicated in
> miniature...the "pickets" are still out, the low challenge of the sentry
> may still be heard, breaking the stillness of the night, but battle has
> not yet been joined.[226]

On April 10, the story became even more interesting:

> A stranger presented himself at the Katalysine Spring yesterday
> evening, after every person had left the grounds except the night
> watchman, who sleeps in one of the buildings, and expressed a desire
> to see the spring and taste the water at its source before leaving in

the morning train. As this is a common occurrence, no suspicion was excited, and he was admitted to the bottling establishment, through which he had to pass in reaching the spring, at that hour. Seizing the opportunity, he thrust his attendant from the building, and following him, turned the key in the door, and coolly informed him that he was an agent of the New York Gettysburg Spring Company, and that he had taken possession for his principals. He occupied the premises during the night, and in the morning quite a crowd assembled, among whom was a large sprinkling of invalids who had come to Gettysburg for water, in anticipation of the stoppage of supplies. Some excitement was evinced, but no disturbance, and peaceable possession was delivered to the resident agent and his employes. The proprietor has notified the Company of his purpose to dispute the right of way to and from the Spring over his land, by demolishing bridges and interposing obstructions. Having accomplished the surprise and recapture of the Spring, the resolute stranger took the cars and returned to New York. He is believed to be a New York detective.[227]

Although Harmon regained possession of the spring shortly after this incident, exactly how he did so is unknown. During the struggle over the spring in early April of 1869, Harmon had surely made enemies in New York City.[228] Meanwhile, work

SHORTLY BEFORE COMPLETION OF THE SPRINGS HOTEL, CONSTRUCTION WORKERS POSED FOR THIS PHOTOGRAPH. ONE MAN APPEARS TO BE DRINKING THE LEGENDARY KATALYSINE WATER. (ACHS)

progressed on the Springs Hotel and the Horse Railway. Dr. G.D. Smith had already hired forty-two carpenters who were hard at work on the hotel's wooden frame. On April 23 local papers announced that a gravel roof would be installed and that a group of painters would soon arrive to work on the building's interior.[229] The *Star and Sentinel* described the hotel in detail:

> The main building fronts North 120 feet and is 44 feet deep, four stories, with an extension from the centre of the main building south 120 by 38 feet four stories. The main entrance will be on the North, with Ladies entrance on the East, a Piaza [sic] 15 feet wide and 200 feet long running the entire front of the building and around the eastern and western ends. The building will accommodate about 300 guests, and will be furnished with all the requisites of a first class Summer Hotel—with a very large Dining and Coltillion [sic] Room, Billiard Room, Bar Room, Reading Room, Ladies' and Gentleman's Parlors...all judiciously arranged with wide halls and corridors.... The Kitchen will be in the rear, with a large Range with capacity to cook for 1000 guests, to meet the demand of future enlargement of the hotel.[230]

In addition to the main building, a cistern and privies were constructed nearby. Ornamental trees, fences, and new roads were also added to transform the property

DETAIL OF PREVIOUS PHOTOGRAPH SHOWING A MAN DRINKING FROM WHAT APPEARS TO BE A BOTTLE OF KATALYSINE WATER. (ACHS)

GEN. GEORGE MEADE ENJOYS KATALYSINE SPRING WATER IN THIS JULY 1869 ILLUSTRATION FROM *LESLIE'S WEEKLY.* THE SPRINGS HOTEL CAN BE SEEN IN THE DISTANCE. (ACHS)

into a recreational park. In June, furniture for the hotel was purchased from some of the finest stores in New York City, Boston, and Philadelphia. At the same time, a group of "first class" black and mulatto waiters were employed by Dr. Smith.[231]

On the evening of June 28, 1869, the Springs Hotel officially opened its doors. On July 1, exactly six years after the bloody struggle took place on the fields of the Harmon farm, the horse-drawn railway was used for the first time. However, "in consequence of the defective condition of the track, growing out of its hurried construction [the cars] did not run smoothly for some days."[232]

That week a number of important guests arrived at the hotel. Among them were Wisconsin governor and former colonel of the 2nd Wisconsin, Lucius Fairchild; Indiana governor Oliver Morton; Gen. George G. Meade and son; Commissioner of Indian Affairs, Ely S. Parker; former divisional commander Gen. Andrew A. Humphreys; and Secretary of War John A. Rawlins.[233]

The hotel thrived throughout the summer of 1869. A gas heating system was installed, and telegraph lines were connected. Around this time Emanuel Harmon leased the spring to a new company, "Plantation Bitters." Soon thereafter bath houses, bathing tubs, and showers were installed use the famous Katalysine spring water.[234]

Gen. Solomon Meredith, former commander of the Iron Brigade, arrived at the hotel during its first week of business. Meredith would have been able to ride the

THIS VIEW OF THE 19TH INDIANA MONUMENT WAS TAKEN FROM WHAT IS NOW MEREDITH
AVENUE. THE SPRINGS HOTEL LAKE IS VISIBLE TO THE LEFT OF THE MEMORIAL. (ACHS)

railway cars to town for a fare of just 10 cents. On August 25 a reunion ball and
reception were held at the hotel, and among the many prominent Union Army
commanders reported to be in attendance were Geary, Slocum, Meredith, Robinson,
Newton, Stone, Stannard, von Steinwehr, Baxter, Howe, Shaler, Greene, Graham,
and McCandless—all legendary names associated with the Battle of Gettysburg. This
was the first major use of the new hotel for veterans' purposes.[235]

AN EARLY STEREO OF THE SPRINGS HOTEL (AIDC)

On August 20 it was announced that George Hoppes would replace Dr. G.D. Smith as manager of the hotel. Hoppes, "one of the best landlords ever known in this part of the country," had been the proprietor of many popular hotels before coming to Gettysburg.[236] In the years to come, Hoppes was responsible for the construction of a new building to be used as a billiard saloon and bowling alley, as well as a new stable and ice house. A lake was created for boating and swimming by damming Willoughby's Run just north of the Mill Road ford. Visible in early photographs of the 19th Indiana Infantry monument, this lake—later removed—existed into the late 1800s.[237]

1870–1917: The Springs Hotel

On June 16, 1870, the *New York Times* ran an extensive story on the spring. At that time, the popularity of the water was at its peak. Scores of visitors flocked to Gettysburg as soon as the hotel opened in June. Among the guests was Adm. John A. Dahlgren, who died suddenly just days after leaving the hotel.[238] The U.S. census taken in August of 1870 indicates that George Hoppes and his family lived on the property. At this time the hotel baker was from Bavaria, Germany, and most of the staff was either mulatto or black.[239]

One form of entertainment at the Springs Hotel during the early 1870s was an Italian band:

> One of the attractive features at the Springs hotel, during the last week, has been the capital music of the band of Italian Minstrels, who, with two violins, and two grand harps and eminent musical talent, daily entertain the guests and visitors.[240]

Despite a change in ownership during the summer of 1871, the hotel continued to thrive under Hoppes's management. In June Edward G. Fahnestock purchased the hotel and its contents for $35,000. "A larger sale... was probably never before made in the county."[241]

In 1871 Emanuel Harmon entered into an agreement with Mrs. S.A. Whitney, "one of the leading members of the wealthy house of Whitney and Co., of Glassboro,

A WHITNEY BOTTLE FROM THE KATALYSINE SPRING (AIDC)

New Jersey." Part of this agreement dealt with production of the bottles for Harmon's spring water. This new model bore the monogram GKW (Gettysburg Katalysine Water) on the front, and "J. Whitney Glass Works Glassboro N.J." on the bottom. The "Whitney Brothers" extensively advertised the water in newspapers all around the country, some ads appearing as far away as Sacramento, California. At the same time, Katalysine water continued to be sold at drug stores in Washington, New York City, Philadelphia, and other major eastern cities.[242]

In May 1872 a veranda was added to the hotel. This porch ran along the entire front of the first story and became a popular destination in its own right.[243] The following year John Bachelder featured the hotel and spring in his travel book *Gettysburg: What to See, and How to see it.* He included a unique illustration depicting the hotel and Horse Railway Bridge over Willoughby's Run. In his Springs Hotel section, he described the view from the hotel veranda:

> Seated at the northeastern corner, facing the east, we have Reynolds' Grove directly in our front, rising above which may be seen the cupola of the Theological Seminary.... In the left foreground are the Springs buildings, over which is a smooth rounded field to the left of Reynolds' Grove.... This vicinity possesses much historic interest. It was here that the battle commenced, and across the field where this house stands that Hill's corps made its first advance; in yonder grove that General Reynolds was killed; and at Willoughby Run that General Archer was captured.[244]

The peacefulness and serenity at the Springs Hotel took a tragic turn one afternoon in early August 1875. Located across Willoughby's Run, just behind the spring, was a deep stone quarry. While gathering blackberries nearby, two children of Mr. Henry Wavell decided to swim in the quarry, which was at that time filled with rainwater. Five-year-old Harry Wavell slipped down the bank and was unable to swim ashore. The second child immediately called for help, and an African-American waiter at the Springs Hotel responded, jumping into the pit in a futile attempt to rescue young Harry. It took nearly 30 minutes to recover the child's body, and "the sad accident awakened a good deal of sympathy among the guests at the Springs Hotel, who promptly contributed... to defray the funeral expenses."[245]

On the morning of February 25, 1876, Emanuel Harmon died in New York City and was buried by "the Masonic order" in Brooklyn's Greenwood Cemetery. At that time, Harmon was in debt to many individuals, especially those representing the Whitney Glass Company which had been manufacturing the bottles for his spring.[246] That same year, Dr. J.W.C. O'Neal published a small booklet about the property that shed some light on Harmon's motives for introducing the spring in 1865: "...the owner proceeded to develop and enlarge [it] as a healing spring and watering place, and thus enable him to repair his losses consequent upon the battle." He further added, "The peculiar disposition of the late proprietor has been rather to sell the water as a popular panacea [an answer to all health problems]...."[247] According to his death certificate, Harmon never married and was living alone at the time of his death. The certificate also indicates that he was "the original inventor of the Gettingsburg [sic] Spring Co."

In 1877 guests at the hotel enjoyed new baths that had been built to utilize the legendary Katalysine water. Additional walks and drives were constructed throughout the property, and the area continued to transform into a respected summer resort complex and battlefield tourism hub.[248]

Tragedy touched the property again on May 17, 1878, when the *Star and Sentinel* reported the accidental drowning of two Lutheran Seminary students in the Springs Hotel Lake.

> It seems that some of the students at the Seminary had organized a boating club and secured control of two boats on the lake, frequently going out to boat for recreation and physical exercise. The lake is shallow, except near the breast of the dam, where the water is nine or ten feet deep. On Wednesday evening six young men went out to the lake.... They got into the two boats near the head of the lake, and while indulging in some sport both boats upset, the occupants being pitched overboard; but as it was a shallow part of the lake, only three feet deep, nothing happened beyond a good wetting...five young men righted the boats, got into them and rowed down toward the southern end of the lake, where the water is deepest...while rowing about somewhat carelessly the boats came into collision, when for some reason Mr. Kohler attempted to jump from his boat into the other—Mr. Metzger at the same time jumping into the boat Kohler had left. Both boats capsized, and all were thrown out into the water...Shindel and Kohler sink [sic] nearly together, and...the last utterance [was]...an exclamation by Mr. Kohler, "I am going, we can't save ourselves" to which Mr. Shindel replied, "Well, if we can't be saved here, God will save us in heaven," and in a few moments the water closed over both.[249]

Although lives had been lost once again at Willoughby's Run, business at the Springs Hotel continued as usual. Before the end of the decade, Henry Yingling became its manager.[250]

A VIEW OF THE SPRINGS HOTEL AFTER THE COMPLETION OF THE VERANDA (SBC)

As the 1880s commenced, the spring continued to be a favorite destination for tourists and veterans alike. Among others, Margaretta Meade, widow of Gen. George Meade, visited the hotel with her children in the summer of 1881.[251] In 1886 a large group of cavalry veterans, including Confederate Gen. Wade Hampton, Union Gen. John B. McIntosh, and "four distinguished representatives of Custer's old command" stayed there. One newspaperman wrote:

> The faces that were then young, and the hair and whiskers that were
> then black, are now furrowed by years and streaked with gray. There
> are crow-foots at the corner of the eyes, but the laughter on their lip
> is hearty and gay.[252]

According to another article, Gen. Hampton was actually "captured" by a detachment of Union cavalry and conveyed to Cemetery Hill where he was "received by the Union veterans with all the honors due to such a distinguished captive."[253] This would be the last year of managing the hotel for Henry Yingling. In May 1887 he was succeeded by Maj. F.W. Coleman, a former hotel keeper in Baltimore.[254]

In 1887 a visit by Mrs. George E. Pickett was also reported:

> The 7.20 train would bring the widow of Gen. Geo. E. Pickett. A
> large crowd gathered about the depot to welcome her, and her tall,

graceful form, attired in black and leaning on the arm of her son, who bears his father's full name, was conspicuous in the crowd. She was escorted by Prof. Henry S. Petty, late of the 17th Virginia regiment, and accompanied by about 40 of the survivors of her husband's command. Taking a carriage she, with her son and escort were driven to the Springs Hotel.[255]

During the summer of 1888, the twenty-fifth anniversary of the Battle of Gettysburg brought many notables to the hotel. Gen. Hiram Berdan, commander of the legendary Berdan Sharpshooters at Gettysburg, wrote: "Comrades: on your arrival in Gettysburg come at once to the Springs Hotel, where you will find tent room and the old flags flying."[256] On July 12 a reporter from the *National Tribune* arrived and found several prominent generals in residence:

> About midnight I decided to try my chances for a 'roost' at the Gettysburg Springs Hotel, a summer resort about two miles from the village. I succeeded in chartering a money-making Pennsylvanian, who had a couple of plow-horses hitched to a dilapidated carriage, to take me thither, the compensation being about what he would get for a day's 'breaking-up' in a stubble-field. I found a notable assembly at the hotel: Sickles, iconic and impressive as he ever is; Slocum, with his refined, scholarly face; Carr, whose brigade did such splendid fighting the second day, and who has since been three times Secretary of State of New York, and will one day be Governor; S. Wiley Crawford, whose division immortalized itself in the Wheatfield...A.G. Curtin, the War Governor of Pennsylvania; H.J. Hunt, Chief of Artillery of the Army of the Potomac; Butterfield, Hooker's and Meade's Chief of Staff; Graham, who fought so stubbornly in the Peach Orchard; Berdan, who sacrificed his gallant sharpshooters in staying Longstreet's charge...Longstreet, after Stonewall Jackson, Lee's most valued and trusted Lieutenant; J.B. Gordon, who commanded a brigade at Gettysburg and a corps at Appomattox...and many others of almost equal note. All were constantly surrounded by groups eager to meet, speak and shake hands with them.... The next morning it was the same, and as the throng gathered on the broad piazzas of the hotel after breakfast the scene was one long to be remembered.[257]

Veterans' reunions at the hotel were not limited to the rooms and porch of the hotel. In 1889 a massive camp was established on the grounds for veterans of the many regiments who had fought just yards away on McPherson's Ridge. In

A LATER VIEW OF THE SPRINGS HOTEL, TAKEN DURING A PERIOD OF VACANCY (ACHS)

attendance were Col. R. Bruce Ricketts, Gen. David M. Gregg, and then-governor of Pennsylvania, James A. Beaver. Veterans of the 149th and 150th Pennsylvania, along with the 17th Pennsylvania Cavalry, made up the majority of the camp.[258]

In the early 1890s, the Springs Hotel continued to welcome guests during the summer months, and Katalysine water was still sold across the nation. A brochure for the hotel assured potential visitors that "a large amount of money is being expended in renovating, painting inside and out…gas, water, baths…and many other new improvements will be added, making it more attractive and comfortable than when first built." The brochure noted that "pure water from a distant spring" would be piped into the building for culinary purposes and "for those who do not require the health-restoring qualities of the Katalysine water." This spring may have been located on the old Herr Farm, or possibly on the Herbst farm across Willoughby's Run.[259]

As 1900 approached and veterans of the Battle of Gettysburg continued to die off, so too did business at the once-bustling Springs Hotel. Companies often went out of business after each summer, and the hotel sat empty for months at a time. During these periods of vacancy, local children would frequently visit the Springs Hotel to explore. Flo Blocher Arnold remembered these adventures:

> I used to call the Springs Hotel, 'My beautiful Golden Castle.' It was deserted no one lived there, only a caretaker who slept nearly all day and allowed us to play at will, provided we behaved like ladies and gentleman…we may have stretched the point often, when we slid

down the bannisters from the fourth floor winding around down-down, gracefully making a smoothe [sic] landing, since there were no newel posts to bring us to an abrupt stop. The hotel was equipped with old fashioned speaking tubes, connecting each room in the hotel with the desk in the lobby, where the guests registered. I can still hear those noisy whistling speaking tubes, as we tried out our voices over them. We roller skated on the long porches and halls and especially in the large deserted ball room with its marble floors and pillars...of course there were other buildings for us to wander through and investigate; there were bath houses, ice houses, laundries and store rooms, barns and several cows.[260]

William G. Weaver also remembered wandering the Harmon farm as a young boy. He wrote that the hotel was "bare and bleak and unoccupied except for a corner of the first floor where the caretaker lived." According to Weaver, the hotel had not been painted in years and was therefore unimpressive, "except for its size." At that time the hotel had been painted yellow, but it is difficult to discern from black and white images what the hotel looked like in previous years.[261] Weaver also recalled a story about the bath houses:

My father told me that when you bathed in the Katalysine water you emerged pure white, and it took some minutes before the pigments of your skin again took on your natural coloring.[262]

In August 1909 a "festival" was held at the Springs Hotel with many Gettysburgians in attendance. Local dairy farmer Carl Griffin, however, was kept from the evening's festivities by an accident at the Springs Hotel bridge, which was at that time only a "foot-log."

Mr. Griffin not being acquainted with the road was following the light of a bicycle just a short distance ahead of him, suddenly the light disappeared behind some bushes when the rider had dismounted to cross the foot-log, the horse belonging to Mr. Griffin is blind of both eyes and stepped over the edge of the abutment before the driver learned of his danger, jumping from the buggy just as it went over the embankment. Mr. Griffin landed in the water below and except for a few bruises escaped uninjured, the masonry from the old bridge has partly crumbled away and the horse falling head first among the stones was badly cut above the temple...about 11 o'clock a second party drove over the same embankment but was very fortunate having escaped without so much as breaking the harness. The old roadway over the bridge to the hotel has been abandoned for a number of years and a wire was stretched across to prevent teams from driving in but the wire had been removed on Saturday night for some purpose and the teams walked heedlessly into the trap.[263]

In 1913 the hotel was reopened for the summer to accommodate veterans and guests for the fiftieth anniversary of the Battle of Gettysburg. The hotel was remodeled and refurbished, and twenty of its 139 rooms were furnished. "The dining room, always attractive, will be put back to its old-time appearance and the kitchen will be fully equipped." An "old well" mentioned in this article is likely the one that still stands just west of the site of the hotel. During this restoration, the spring was "thoroughly cleaned and the medicinal water...will again be featured as one of the attractions of the place."[264] In June a gas explosion in the basement of the hotel injured two Gettysburg residents, but the structure was not significantly damaged. This would be one of the last times that the Springs Hotel opened its doors to guests.[265]

The following year a new bridge was added over Willoughby's Run to make passage to the Springs Hotel safer. Things were winding down by 1916, when what

AN EARLY 1900S VIEW OF WILLOUGHBY'S RUN NEAR WHERE CARL GRIFFIN'S ACCIDENT TOOK PLACE (ACHS)

remained of the Springs Hotel furniture was sold at a public auction. In June of 1917 the hotel opened once again, likely for the last time, to house carpenters who were building a training camp for World War I recruits on the field of "Pickett's Charge."[266]

An era ended just before noon on December 17, 1917, when a fire started in a wall of the hotel. David Sterner, the caretaker of the property, left quickly, unable to stop the fire himself. A recent snowstorm had prevented firemen from reaching the property. The *Gettysburg Times* described the scene:

> The blaze when first discovered was in the rear portion of the building but it soon spread throughout the entire structure and burned rapidly until the old frame building was a roaring mass of flames. Wide halls helped to make drafts which fanned the fire and it was little more than half an hour from the time the fire was first seen until it had spread into every nook and corner of the big structure. It made a wonderful sight for it progressed so rapidly that the flames were shooting up around the cupola before any part of the building had fallen and the place was practically all ablaze at one time. The flames mounted high into the air and the fire could be seen from a great distance. Persons living in that section drove over the drifted roads and through fields to witness the spectacle but things were so badly drifted that comparatively few reached the place until it was down.[267]

THIS 1930S PHOTOGRAPH OF THE HARMON FARM WAS TAKEN FROM THE FORMER ABRAHAM SPANGLER FARM ALONG THE CHAMBERSBURG PIKE. (SCMLGC)

At the time of the fire Calvin Gilbert of Gettysburg owned the hotel, which was "standing idle, a monument to the good times of bygone days."[268] Three years later, Gilbert advertised the 111-acre property and eventually sold it at a public sale. He asserted that a large amount of "stone building material" was still present in the hotel foundation and that a "substantial covering structure," probably the original springhouse was located over the spring. Gilbert also offered the 43-acre Springs Hotel Woods at public sale, and it was purchased by the National Park Service in 1920. At that time the woods consisted of oak and hickory trees which had apparently never been cleared.[269]

Although the grand old hotel was gone, there was still potential for the Katalysine Spring. A man named Clyde D. Berger would try his best to rekindle its popularity.

1917–47: New Bottling Works

After lying dormant since the great fire of 1917, the Katalysine Spring was once more abuzz with activity. On May 11, 1935, the *Gettysburg Compiler* announced that the famous Katalysine spring would soon reopen, and that the new owner, Clyde Berger, had big plans for the property. A stone building, made partly from materials "resurrected from the foundation of the old Springs hotel" was already being built. It would be 102 feet long and would house a bottling plant for Berger's spring water.[270] This structure still stands several hundred yards south of the Chambersburg Pike on what was once part of the Abraham Spangler farm. Berger

A VIEW OF THE 1930S BOTTLING ESTABLISHMENT. THIS BUILDING, ALTHOUGH MUCH LARGER, STILL STANDS NEAR THE CHAMBERSBURG PIKE. (SCMLGC)

laid copper pipe to carry the water straight from the spring to his new bottling plant.
At the same time, the old Springs Hotel farm was greatly improved:

> The 140-acre property is undergoing a complete "cleaning." Much of
> the wooded tract has been cleared. The Katalysine spring has been
> cleared, cleaned and restored to its natural and former attraction. A
> large portion of the tract has been plowed and sodded. New roads are
> being constructed and within the early future the once popular resort
> place of Gettysburg, located on the battlefield, will be the scene of
> considerable activity.[271]

Berger announced that the land would become a public park and that he would
eventually dam Willoughby's Run to recreate the Springs Hotel Lake. An estimated
$20,000 was being spent to rejuvenate the property. Berger shipped water to
California, New York, and New Jersey in order to rebuild interest in his spring. In
June he offered the water at a "reduced price" of 25 cents per gallon and encouraged
everyone to "learn from the actual usage the benefits to be derived from using the
famous Katalysine Mineral Springs Water."[272]

In late July and early August of 1935, new bottle-washing machines were installed

SOME OF THE NEW MACHINERY AND COPPER PIPE INSTALLED BY CLYDE BERGER INSIDE HIS
BOTTLING WORKS (SCMLGC)

in Berger's stone building, and the spring's walls were rebuilt to conform with state and federal standards. Berger planned to landscape the entire property and create a "public park and playground," complete with tennis courts and a nine-hole golf course. He launched an advertising campaign for the spring, publishing booklets, brochures, and weekly newspaper advertisements. He even designated a week in August as "Katalysine Week" and once again offered the water at a reduced price.[273]

From 1936 to 1940 the water was continually advertised and sold at the bottling plant on the Chambersburg Pike. But Berger's attempt to recapture public interest didn't last. Ads disappeared from the local newspapers by 1940, and business dwindled. In 1947 Berger gave up on his investment and sold the property to a group of Gettysburgians who planned to transform it into a nine-hole golf course. The Gettysburg Country Club was born.[274]

A 1937 AERIAL PHOTOGRAPH OF THE HARMON FARM (PGS)

DETAIL OF THE 1937 AERIAL PHOTOGRAPH SHOWING DEBRIS FROM THE SPRINGS HOTEL (PGS)

Epilogue

1947–2011: A President and his Golf Course

> With the purchase Saturday of the old Springs Hotel property, also
> known as Katalysine Springs, on Lincolnway west, seven-tenths of a
> mile from Gettysburg, by a group of Adams county residents, work
> will begin immediately on a new golf course and country club on
> this site, to be known as the Gettysburg Country Club.[275]

Although creating a golf course on the property had been suggested by Mr. Berger nearly a decade earlier, it wasn't until the spring of 1947 that the project was taken up by a group of twenty-six Gettysburg businessmen. Calling themselves the "Gettysburg Development Corporation," the group finalized the purchase of Berger's land on October 18, 1947, for $19,000.[276]

The nine-hole course was "laid out immediately, to be ready for use in the spring of 1948." Improvements to the property would also include tennis courts, a skeet range, and a swimming pool "constructed to utilize the waters of the famous springs." (To the author's knowledge, this plan for the swimming pool apparently never materialized.)[277]

The old Berger Bottling Works building soon became the Country Club's Lower Clubhouse, and the bottling equipment was removed to make room for lockers, a golf shop, and recreational rooms: "The building is said to be in excellent condition, with a large fireplace."[278]

It was reported that the Country Club would also create a pond for fishing and winter skating by building a new "off-channel dam." This pond, installed in August 1947, held a staggering 1,000,000 gallons of water, most of which was collected from tributaries of Willoughby's Run and from the spring itself.[279]

Sometime during the next decade, Country Club Lane was built on the eastern edge of the Springs Hotel Woods. This path originally belonged to the Country Club

PRESIDENT DWIGHT D. EISENHOWER PREPARES FOR A LONG ROUND OF GOLF AT THE GETTYSBURG COUNTRY CLUB. (ENHS)

but was later turned over to Cumberland Township. New homes soon sprang up along this road.[280]

In late 1947 the Country Club acquired a smaller tract northwest of the old bottling works building on the Chambersburg Pike on which The Terrace Restaurant had operated. This building became known as the Upper Clubhouse.[281]

Throughout the summer and fall of 1947, crews worked to complete the nine-hole golf course. In the process, portions of the Springs Hotel foundation were covered by sand traps and greens, and historic topographical features were destroyed. Eventually homes were built on the former site of the Harmon house. By this time the spring had long since been permanently closed.

On July 13, 1948, the *Gettysburg Times* announced that the Gettysburg Country Club was open for business with its new pool and golf course.[282]

Over the next several decades improvements were made to the property. In the 1950s a ring for racing and training horses was installed just north of the spring, and a concrete-block barn for housing the horses was built south of the track. (This structure was later used to store golf carts.) A horseback riding trail was created from the barn to the Mill Road, and another horse ring was installed south of the Mill Road on the former Stallsmith farm.[283] In 1953 a small building was erected north of the "Lower Club House." This building became the Ladies Locker Room and was used as a lifeguard station in the early 2000s.[284]

Things changed at the Club on the afternoon of April 2, 1955, with the arrival of a very special golfer—President Dwight D. Eisenhower:

> The President drove to the club from his farm at 1:30 P.M., stepped out
> of his car, changed his shoes, took five or six practice shots on the
> putting green and then teed off without a warmup.[285]

Eisenhower became a regular at the club during the next four years, receiving an honorary membership from the club president. Ike's Secret Service agents carried their own golf bags, fitted out with walkie-talkies and weapons to protect the President. One summer Eisenhower golfed there so frequently that he accidentally crashed "Ladies Day." On another occasion he was interrupted while playing the second hole.

> A playful tan and white dog almost broke up President Eisenhower's
> golf game yesterday. The dog grabbed the President's golf ball
> ...waged [sic] his tail at the President and loped off gleefully. Secret
> Service guards took off after the little dog and managed to wheedle
> the ball away from him. Mr. Eisenhower continued his game and
> played 27 holes for the first time since the day before his heart attack
> in Denver last Sept.[286]

Eisenhower typically arrived "dressed all in blue—cap, sports shirt, and slacks," accompanied by his old friend, Brig. Gen. Arthur S. Nevins, or by his grandson, David, who appears in many press photographs on the course.[287]

Eisenhower was never too pleased with his golf game. Just before teeing off one day he was heard to say: "An old man takes a long time limbering up." He usually played twenty-seven holes—three times around the course.[288]

For the next fifty years the Gettysburg Country Club prospered. During this time more houses were built along Country Club Lane and the Old Mill Road. In the 1970s the old Stallsmith farm became the Twin Lakes development, and the Stallsmith buildings were eventually demolished. Despite several attempts by the National

PRESIDENT EISENHOWER AND HIS GRANDSON, DAVID, BEGIN A ROUND OF GOLF AT THE GETTYSBURG COUNTRY CLUB. (ENHS)

Park Service to "trade" the land and open it up for development—attempts that were thwarted by battlefield enthusiasts and historians—the Springs Hotel Woods has remained in the hands of the National Park Service for more than 90 years.

In 2008, after constructing a new clubhouse and tennis courts, the Gettysburg Country Club declared bankruptcy. The land was eventually acquired by Martin Hill, who shortly thereafter subdivided it. This division removed the pool and tennis courts from the golf course, the latter being of primary interest to the National Park Service. After nearly 150 years, the Harmon farm was destined to become part of the Gettysburg National Military Park. Negotiations with Mr. Hill resulted in the sale of the 95-acre Harmon farm to the Conservation Fund and the Civil War Trust, clearing the way for the final transfer of the property to the National Park Service.

A New Addition

On March 25, 2011, a group of Park Service officials, leaders of preservation organizations, and Interior Secretary Ken Salazar met on the fields of the Harmon farm. After a brief ceremony, the property was formally transferred to the Park Service, protecting it forever from further development. Secretary Salazar spoke briefly:

> Gettysburg will always have a sacred place in America's heritage for the pivotal role it played in our nation's history and for the enormity of the sacrifice that took place here... with the addition of the Emanuel Harman farm to the Gettysburg National Military Park, we are able to include another important chapter in the story that helped shape our country.[289]

Appendix 1: Units engaged on or near the Harmon Farm, July 1, 1863

Union Army of the Potomac: Maj. Gen. George G. Meade

First Corps *Maj. Gen. John F. Reynolds (Maj. Gen. Abner Doubleday)*

First Division *Brig. Gen. James S. Wadsworth*

First Brigade *Brig. Gen. Solomon Meredith*

2nd Wisconsin Infantry *Col. Lucius Fairchild*

7th Wisconsin Infantry *Col. William W. Robinson*

19th Indiana Infantry *Col. Samuel J. Williams*

24th Michigan Infantry *Col. Henry A. Morrow*

Third Division *Brig. Gen. Thomas A. Rowley*

First Brigade *Col. Chapman Biddle*

80th New York Infantry (20th New York State Militia) *Col. Theodore B. Gates*

121st Pennsylvania Infantry *Maj. Alexander Biddle*

142nd Pennsylvania Infantry *Col. Robert P. Cummins*

151st Pennsylvania Infantry *Lt. Col. George F. McFarland*

Second Brigade *Col. Roy Stone*

150th Pennsylvania Infantry *Col. Langhorne Wister*

Artillery Brigade *Col. Charles S. Wainwright*

1st Pennsylvania Light Artillery, Battery B *Capt. James H. Cooper*

Cavalry Corps *Maj. Gen. Alfred Pleasonton*

First Division *Brig. Gen. John Buford*

First Brigade *Col. William Gamble*

8th Illinois Cavalry *Maj. John L. Beveridge*

8th New York Cavalry *Lt. Col. William L. Markell*

Confederate Army of Northern Virginia: Gen. Robert E. Lee

Third Corps *Lt. Gen. Ambrose P. Hill*

Heth's Division *Maj. Gen. Henry Heth*

First Brigade *Brig. Gen. James J. Pettigrew*

11th North Carolina Infantry *Col. Collett Leventhorpe*

26th North Carolina Infantry *Col. Henry K. Burgwyn, Jr.*

47th North Carolina Infantry *Col. George H. Faribault*

52nd North Carolina Infantry *Col. James K. Marshall*

Second Brigade *Col. John M. Brockenbrough*

    40th Virginia Infantry *Capt. T. E. Betts*

    47th Virginia Infantry *Col. Robert M. Mayo*

    55th Virginia Infantry *Col. William S. Christian*

    22nd Virginia Infantry Battalion *Maj. John S. Bowles*

Third Brigade *Brig. Gen. James Jay Archer*

    13th Alabama Infantry *Col. Birkett D. Fry*

    5th Alabama Infantry Battalion *Maj. A. S. Van de Graaff*

    1st Tennessee Infantry (Provisional Army) *Maj. Felix G. Buchanan*

    7th Tennessee Infantry *Lt. Col. Samuel G. Shepard*

    14th Tennessee Infantry *Capt. Bruce L. Phillips*

Pender's Division *Maj. Gen. William Dorsey Pender*

First Brigade *Col. Abner Perrin*

    1st South Carolina Infantry (Provisional Army) *Maj. Charles W. McCreary*

    12th South Carolina Infantry *Col. John L. Miller*

    13th South Carolina Infantry *Lt. Col. Benjamin T. Brockman*

    14th South Carolina Infantry *Lt. Col. Joseph N. Brown*

Second Brigade *Brig. Gen. James H. Lane*

    7th North Carolina Infantry *Capt. J. McLeod Turner*

    18th North Carolina Infantry *Col. John D. Barry*

    28th North Carolina Infantry *Col. Samuel D. Lowe*

    33rd North Carolina Infantry *Col. Clark M. Avery*

    37th North Carolina Infantry *Col. William M. Barbour*

Fourth Brigade *Brig. Gen. Alfred M. Scales*

    13th North Carolina Infantry *Col. Joseph H. Hyman*

    16th North Carolina Infantry *Capt. Leroy W. Stowe*

    22nd North Carolina Infantry *Col. James Conner*

    34th North Carolina Infantry *Col. William Lee J. Lowrance*

    38th North Carolina Infantry *Col. William J. Hoke*

Appendix 2: A Photographic Mystery

The exact location of the three following 1867 views is currently unknown to historians.[290] Captions from the original stereo photographs indicate simply that they were taken along the banks of Willoughby's Run in close proximity to the Katalysine Spring. One could surmise that the woodlot visible in the distant background of the photograph immediately below is either Herbst Woods or the Springs Hotel Woods.

There are several logical explanations as to why the current topography of the land has prevented historians from identifying where these photographs were taken. Much of the land on both sides of Willoughby's Run has been drastically altered since the spring of 1867 when Charles J. Tyson or one of his employees ventured out to the creek with his photographic equipment. At that time the land on both sides of the creek rose abruptly. Because of subsequent development of the Springs Hotel Lake, much of the land south of Herbst Woods does not appear as it did in the

AN UNIDENTIFIED MAN GAZES ACROSS WILLOUGHBY'S RUN. NOTE THE WOODLOT AND FENCE IN THE DISTANT BACKGROUND. (FRASSANITO COLL.)

1860s. North of Herbst Woods, the Gettysburg Country Club created its horse racing ring, and later a driving range, on the west bank of the stream. As this area appears today to be unnaturally flat, it is evident that bulldozers destroyed the original topography during the development of the golf course.

One might argue that despite these changes in elevation, the rock that appears in all three photographs must surely still exist along the side of the creek. Herein lies the mystery: No such rock has been found in spite of tireless efforts by historians William A. Frassanito and Timothy H. Smith. It is the author's theory that the rock may have been used for the foundation of the Springs Hotel. The following account helps to support this idea:

A VARIANT OF THE FIRST PHOTOGRAPH, FEATURING THE SAME UNIDENTIFIED MAN (FRASSANITO COLL.)

...the formation of rocks beneath the soil, around this spring...are in form and sizes fit for the builder on removal therefrom. We have seen some of these stones thrown from their beds by the explosive force of gun-powder which could be laid by the Mason without the use of pick or adze.... Nature has here provided for the realization of one of the wonders of ancient art.[291]

Although this explanation offers a possible solution to the mystery, the author encourages his readers to venture beyond the run and investigate for themselves.

A VIEW SHOWING CHARLIE KRAUTH, GRANDSON OF THE FIRST PRESIDENT OF GETTYSBURG COLLEGE, TAKEN A SHORT DISTANCE FROM THE TWO PREVIOUS VIEWS (ACHS)

Appendix 3: The Family of Amelia Evelyn Harmon

George W. Miller

Pennsylvania Methodist church records state that George Washington Miller was born on April 4, 1845 near Gettysburg, Pennsylvania. On August 10, 1862, he enlisted in Company A, 6th Maryland Infantry. Two years later he was seriously wounded in Virginia at the Battle of the Wilderness on May 5, 1864. "[He] carried in his body until his death a slug of lead received in battle." According to his obituary in *The New York Times* (November 30, 1930), Miller "studied for the Methodist ministry in a convalescent camp. He preached his first sermon from an invalid's rolling chair and later became known as 'the boy orator of Maryland.'" After the war, Miller was involved with the Methodist Church in Gettysburg, where he met and married Amelia E. Harmon in 1868. For the next five decades Amelia and George lived in numerous places where George had been assigned as a clergyman. They had four children. By 1930 George was a widower. At that time he lived with his daughter Jewell and her family. He died on November 29, 1930, at age 86, at the Methodist Episcopal Hospital in Brooklyn, New York.

Children of Amelia Harmon and George Miller

Maud A. Miller, born June 20, 1869, in Selinsgrove, Snyder County, Pennsylvania. She married a man whose surname was Hipple. In 1937 Maud traveled to England and Italy. Ship records help to clarify her date of birth and birthplace. On the 1930 census her occupation is listed as school teacher.

R. Eugene Miller, born about 1871 in Pennsylvania.

Jewell Martha Miller, born October 5, 1876, in Bellefonte, Pennsylvania. She married Ferdinand Pfaltz in about 1899. They had at least two children (see below).

Grace E. Miller, born August 19, 1882, in Wilmington, Delaware. In 1905 she married Arthur C. Stott in Annapolis, Maryland. The following wedding announcement appeared in the *New York Tribune* on February 3, 1905:

> PASSED MIDSHIPMAN MARRIES. Special Permission Granted by Secretary of the Navy for the Wedding. The wedding of Miss Grace E. Miller, daughter of the Rev. George W. Miller, pastor of the First Methodist Episcopal Church here, to Passed Midshipman Arthur C. Stott, of Stottsville, N. Y., took place to-day in the church of which her father is pastor. The service was performed by Dr. Miller....

Grace Miller Stott died December 20, 1968, in La Jolla, San Diego County, California. She is buried there in El Camino Memorial Park. Census records indicate that she had no children.

Known Grandchildren of Amelia Harmon and George Miller

Albert Ferdinand Pfaltz, born about 1903 in New York. He married a woman named Hazle sometime before 1940.

Helen Jewell Pfaltz, born about 1908 in New York.

Notes

[1]1858 Adams County Map, Adams County Historical Society.

[2]Kathleen Georg Harrison, *The Significance of the Harmon Farm and the Springs Hotel Woods*, p. 2, Harmon Farm Vertical File, Gettysburg National Military Park; U.S. Direct Tax of 1798; 1810 United States Federal Census, Cumberland Township, Adams County, Pennsylvania.

[3]Kathleen Georg Harrison, *The Significance of the Harmon Farm and the Springs Hotel Woods*, p. 3, GNMP Harmon Farm Vertical File.

[4]Ibid.

[5]Colonel Jacob M. Sheads, *The Burning of the Home of General "Stonewall" Jackson's Uncle by the Rebels During the First Day's Battle of Gettysburg, July 1, 1863*, GNMP Harmon Farm Vertical File.

[6]Kathleen Georg Harrison, *The Significance of the Harmon Farm and the Springs Hotel Woods*, p. 3, GNMP; D.X. Junkin, *The Reverend George Junkin, D.D., LL.D. A Historical Biography*, p. 57.

[7]Colonel Jacob M. Sheads, *The Burning of the Home of General "Stonewall" Jackson's Uncle by the Rebels*, GNMP; *Adams Sentinel*, January 25, 1841.

[8]*Adams Sentinel*, January 25, 1841.

[9]Kathleen Georg Harrison, *The Significance of the Harmon Farm and the Springs Hotel Woods*, p. 3, GNMP; Colonel Jacob M. Sheads, *The Burning of the Home of General "Stonewall" Jackson's Uncle by the Rebels*, GNMP; *Adams Sentinel*, July 23, 1860; *Adams Sentinel*, January 2, 1861.

[10]Kathleen Georg Harrison, *The Significance of the Harmon Farm and the Springs Hotel Woods*, p. 3, GNMP; 1850 United States Federal Census, Cumberland Township, Adams County, Pennsylvania.

[11]This is likely the same structure that was advertised by Reverend McLean as a "large log tenant house." The site of this building is just west of current Park Avenue; Keefauver appears on Cumberland Township tax lists from 1862-1867 and probably farmed the Stallsmith property for the greater portion of this time period. See Adams County Tax Records, ACHS.

[12]Kathleen Georg Harrison, *The Significance of the Harmon Farm and the Springs Hotel Woods*, GNMP.

[13]Ibid. Library of Congress, *Biographical Directory of the United States Congress*; 1858 Adams County Map, ACHS.

[14]After viewing Emanuel Harmon's signature on many documents it is clear that he spelled his name with an O, as in "Harmon," as opposed to the incorrect spelling: "Harman." For the rest of the Harmon family, the spelling seems to have been interchangeable.

[15]New York City Death Index online; the 1870 Septennial Census for Cumberland Township, Adams County, indicates that he was born several years later than 1818.

[16]United States Patent Office, Patent Number 6,241.

[17]Kathleen Georg Harrison, *The Significance of the Harmon Farm and the Springs Hotel Woods*, p. 5, GNMP; *Adams Sentinel*, March 5, 1862.

[18]United States Patent Office, Patent Numbers 12,161; 13,838; 23,300; 39,569; and 41,991.

[19]Delaware state birth record for Grace Miller, daughter of Amelia E. Harmon, August 19, 1882 (found at www.familysearch.com), *Adams Sentinel*, December 8, 1863: This article states that Amelia is the daughter of "R.T. Harmon"; 1850 United States Federal Census, Warrington Township, York County, Pennsylvania; Last Will and Testament of Abraham Harmon, York County Historical Society Estate Files: This is the will of Amelia Harmon's grandfather. He mentions his son "Tydings Richard"; Civil War Pension record for Richard T. Harman, Independent Battery B, Pennsylvania Light Artillery; headstone of Henry L. Camp, unknown location, www.findagrave.com. The headstone indicates that Camp married Amelia Jewell in Louisiana in 1832; 1850 United States Federal Census, Warrington Township, York County, Pennsylvania, there is a seven year old "Emma Camp" on this census record, indicating a connection between the Harmon and Camp families; 1910 United States Federal Census, Asbury Park Ward 2, Monmouth County, New Jersey: This record indicates that Amelia Harmon's mother was born in Louisiana; 1880 Census, Wilmington, New Castle, Delaware: This record states that Amelia Harmon named one of her daughters "Jewell." With all of these clues, and further evidence from www.ancestry.com, the author is convinced that Amelia Harmon's mother was Amelia Jewell Camp, of Louisiana.

[20]*Biographical Index of the graduates of the Homeopathic Medical College of Pennsylvania and the Hahnemann Medical College and Hospital of Philadelphia*, p. 142.

[21]1850 United States Federal Census, Warrington Township, York County, Pennsylvania.

[22]Ibid. 1860 United States Federal Census, Cumberland Township, Adams County, Pennsylvania. This record shows that R.T. was briefly living in the Harmon house with his new wife, Caroline, and their children; *Adams Sentinel*, December 8, 1863.

[23]1860 United States Federal Census, Cumberland Township, Adams County, Pennsylvania.

[24]*The Water Cure Journal*, May, 1852.

[25]*Adams Sentinel*, December 8, 1863; 1850 United States Federal Census, Warrington Township, York County, Pennsylvania; Civil War pension record for Richard T. Harmon, Independent Battery B, Pennsylvania Light Artillery (found at www.fold3.com).

[26]*Compiler*, July 3, 1915.

[27]1870 United States Federal Census, Cumberland Township, Adams County, Pennsylvania.

[28]Damage Claim of William Comfort, GNMP Damage Claims Files; Last Will and Testament of Abraham Harmon, York County Historical Society Estate Files.

[29]1850 United States Federal Census, Warrington Township, York County, Pennsylvania; *Adams Sentinel*, December 8, 1863.

[30]*Compiler*, July 3, 1915.

[31]Soldier's Diary, 8th New York Vertical File, GNMP; William L. Markell account, from New York at Gettysburg, p. 1145.

[32]F.S. Harris, "Gen. Jas. J. Archer," *Confederate Veteran Magazine*, Volume 3, p. 18.

[33]Dr. W.H. Moon, "Beginning of the Battle at Gettysburg," *Confederate Veteran Magazine*, Volume 33, pp. 449–450.

[34]There is some debate as to which regiment occupied the right flank of Archer's brigade. Dr. Moon of the 13th Alabama wrote upon being ordered to retreat later that morning: "we could see no reason for the order." If the 13th Alabama was on the right of the brigade, it is strange that soldiers of the regiment were unaware of a massive flank attack on their own regiment. Members of the Iron Brigade also mentioned that a Tennessee regiment was on the right of Archer's line. Finally, John Bachelder, a meticulous early historian and mapmaker at Gettysburg, placed the 1st Tennessee on the right of Archer's line, and was praised by Col. Birkett Fry of the 13th Alabama for the map's accuracy. Respected historian Timothy H. Smith has argued that this alignment is correct based on the above evidence.

[35]Letter of A.S. Van de Graaff to his wife, July 8, 1863, 5th Alabama Battalion Vertical File, GNMP.

[36]Moon, "Beginning of the Battle at Gettysburg." The terrain today is much as Moon described.

[37]OR Part 2, p. 646.

[38]Moon, "Beginning of the Battle at Gettysburg," *Confederate Veteran Magazine*, Volume 33, pp. 449–450.

[39]John H. Calef, "Gettysburg Notes: The Opening Gun," *Journal of the Military Service Institution of the United States*, Volume 40, p. 48.

[40]Ibid., p.48.

[41]Moon, "Beginning of the Battle at Gettysburg," pp. 449-450.

[42]Ibid. OR Part 2, p. 646.

[43]The "Iron Brigade" will hereafter be referred to without quotation marks. The brigade was made up of "western" regiments: three from Wisconsin, one from Michigan, and one from Indiana. In previous battles they had earned the nickname "Iron Brigade" because of their ferocity in combat.

[44]*Compiler*, July 3, 1915.

[45]OR Part 2, p. 646.

[46] J.H. Stine, "History of the Army of the Potomac," pp. 458–459.

[47] Letter of D.B. Daily, 2nd Wisconsin Infantry, March 24, 1890, 2nd Wisconsin Vertical File, GNMP.

[48] OR Part 2, p. 646.

[49] Robert K. Beecham, "The Pivotal Battle of the Civil War," pp. 66–69.

[50] OR Part 1, pp. 267–273.

[51] J.B. Turney, "The First Tennessee at Gettysburg," *Confederate Veteran Magazine*, Volume 8, p. 535.

[52] Moon, "Beginning of the Battle at Gettysburg."

[53] W.H. Bird, *Stories of the Civil War*, pp.6–8.

[54] OR Part 2, p. 646.

[55] John B. Bachelder Maps, ACHS.

[56] Report of Colonel Robert M. Mayo, 47th Virginia Infantry, August 13, 1863, 47th Virginia Vertical File, GNMP.

[57] Jaquelin M. Meredith, "The First Day at Gettysburg," *Southern Historical Society Papers*, Volume 24, p. 184.

[58] Orson B. Curtis, *History of the Twenty-Fourth Michigan of the Iron Brigade*, p. 157.

[59] OR Part 1, pp. 267–273.

[60] Official Report of Col. Samuel J. Williams, 19th Indiana Infantry, printed in *Gettysburg Magazine*, Volume 2, pp. 29–31.

[61] John. R. Callis to John B. Bachelder, 7th Wisconsin Vertical File, GNMP.

[62] Beecham, *The Pivotal Battle of the Civil War*, p. 67. Bryan is buried in Pleasant Hill Cemetery, Hughesville, Pennsylvania.

[63] OR Part 1, pp. 267–273.

[64] John B. Bachelder Maps, ACHS. This alignment is widely accepted among historians. Another regiment of the Iron Brigade, the 6th Wisconsin Infantry, had been detached early in the day and fought primarily alongside General Lysander Cutler's brigade.

[65] OR Part 2, pp. 642-644.

[66] Walter Clark, *Histories of the Several Regiments and Battalions from North Carolina in the Great War 1861-65*, Volume 2, p. 348.

[67] Calculated by the author using the total strength of each regiment and the number of feet that each unit occupied while in line of battle.

[68] OR Part 2, pp. 642-644.

[69] Account of W.M. McCall, 7th Tennessee Infantry, *Confederate Veteran Magazine*, Volume 3, p. 19; OR Part 2, p. 646.

[70] J.B. Turney, "The First Tennessee at Gettysburg," *Confederate Veteran Magazine*, Volume 8, p. 535.

[71] George H. Chapman to John B. Bachelder, March 30, 1864, in *The Bachelder Papers*, Volume 1, p. 130; Account of John L. Beveridge in *Illinois Monuments at Gettysburg*, p. 21.

[72] John Bachelder Maps, ACHS. This path is now "Willoughby Run Road."

[73] Marcellus Jones Journal, 8th Illinois Vertical File, GNMP.

[74] Letter to John P. Nicholson, December 9, 1918, Storrick Collection, ACHS. This account was brought to light by historian Timothy H. Smith, who recently discovered the letter in a box at the Adams County Historical Society that had not been opened for many years.

[75] Historian Seward R. Osborne suggested this route in his book, *Holding the Left at Gettysburg*. Many accounts from Biddle's brigade mention arriving on the Fairfield/Hagerstown Road near Willoughby's Run.

[76] John D.S. Cook, "Personal Reminiscences of Gettysburg," from *War Talks in Kansas*, p. 324.

[77] *Pennsylvania at Gettysburg*, Volume 2, p. 660.

[78] Col. Theodore B. Gates, *The Ulster Guard [20th N.Y. State Militia] and the War of the Rebellion*, p. 432.

[79] Cook, "Personal Reminiscences of Gettysburg," from *War Talks in Kansas*, p. 324.

[80] Col. Theodore B. Gates to John B. Bachelder, January 30, 1864, *The Bachelder Papers*, Volume 2, pp. 80–82. In his book Gates wrote: "crossing Willoughby Run between the road and the house of D. Finneprock [*sic*], around which Buford's dismounted cavalry were skirmishing." In his letter to Bachelder, Gates did not identify the buildings but wrote, "I was ordered to throw out a company of skirmishers to occupy the house and buildings already spoken of." Therefore, in both accounts he must be referring to the Harmon house, which was occupied at the time of the battle by David Finefrock. After the battle, David and Rachel Finefrock moved to the Stallsmith house, which is why the Warren map identifies this farm as "D. Finnefrock;" miscellaneous account, 149th Pennsylvania Vertical File, GNMP. This account was brought to the author's attention by Timothy H. Smith.

[81] Col. Theodore B. Gates, *The Ulster Guard [20th N.Y. State Militia] and the War of the Rebellion*, pp. 432–433.

[82] Col. Theodore B. Gates to John B. Bachelder, January 30, 1864, *The Bachelder Papers*, Volume 1, pp. 80–82.

[83] Enos B. Vail, *Reminiscences of a Boy in the Civil War*, p. 127.

[84] Cook, "Personal Reminiscences of Gettysburg," from *War Talks in Kansas*, p. 325.

[85] *History of the 121st Regiment Pennsylvania Volunteers, an Account from the Ranks*, p. 228.

[86]Vail, *Reminiscences of a Boy in the Civil War*, pp. 127-128.

[87]Seward R. Osborne, *Holding the Left at Gettysburg, The 20th New York State Militia on July 1, 1863*, p. 8.

[88]Vail, *Reminiscences of a Boy in the Civil War*, p. 127.

[89]Gates, *The Ulster Guard [20th N.Y. State Militia] and the War of the Rebellion*, p. 433; Vail, *Reminiscences of a Boy in the Civil War*, p. 127.

[90]*Compiler*, July 3, 1915.

[91]Clark, *Histories of the Several Regiments*, Volume 3, p. 236.

[92]Ibid., p. 105.

[93]*Charlotte Daily Observer*, July 4, 1903; for more information on Henry Burgwyn, see *Boy Colonel of the Confederacy, the Life and Times of Henry King Burgwyn, Jr.* by Archie K. Davis.

[94]*Charlotte Daily Observer*, July 4, 1903.

[95]Clark, *Histories of the Several Regiments*, Volume 2, p. 350.

[96]Ibid., pp. 368–369.

[97]Cook, "Personal Reminiscences of Gettysburg," from *War Talks in Kansas*, pp. 325–326.

[98]Gates, *The Ulster Guard [20th N.Y. State Militia] and the War of the Rebellion*, p. 433; Seward R. Osborne, *Holding the Left at Gettysburg*, p. 11. According to Mr. Osborne's calculations, a total of 72 men from companies K and G were positioned at the Harmon farm at this time. Volunteers like Alexander Tice would have further bolstered this number.

[99]Report of Colonel Robert M. Mayo, 47th Virginia Infantry, August 13, 1863, 47th Virginia Vertical File, GNMP.

[100]The Bucktail Brigade consisted of three Pennsylvania regiments: The 143rd, the 149th, and the 150th. Members of the brigade pinned deer tails to their hats to distinguish themselves from other units. They were often referred to as the "Bogus Bucktails" because they were not the first Union soldiers to sport this distinctive attire. See GNMP Vertical Files for more information.

[101]*Pennsylvania at Gettysburg*, Volume 2, p. 734.

[102]Ibid., p. 735.

[103]Henry Heth to S. Cooper, October 13, 1864, 22nd Virginia Battalion Vertical File, GNMP.

[104]OR Part 2, p. 670; OR Part 1, pp. 273–275.

[105]Clark, *Histories of the Several Regiments*, Volume 2, p. 351.

[106]*Charlotte Daily Observer*, July 4, 1903; interview with John R. Lane, W.H.S. Burgwyn Papers, copy in 26th North Carolina Vertical File, GNMP.

[107]Mrs. B.A.C. Emerson, "The Most Famous Regiment," *Confederate Veteran Magazine*, Volume 25, pp. 352–355.

[108]*Charlotte Daily Observer*, July 4, 1903.

[109]Ibid.

[110]W.B. Taylor letter, July 29, 1863, 11th North Carolina Vertical File, GNMP.

[111]Ibid., J.W.C. O'Neal Burial Journal, GNMP Library.

[112]Colonel Leventhorpe wrote: "I had my left arm shattered by a Minie ball, and was badly hit on the hip also, & carried off the field." For more information, see *Collett Leventhorpe, the English Confederate*, by J. Timothy Cole and Bradley R. Foley.

[113]Clark, *Histories of the Several Regiments*, Volume 3, p. 106.

[114]*Compiler*, July 3, 1915.

[115]Michael W. Taylor, "Col. James Keith Marshall: One of Three Brigade Commanders Killed in the Pickett-Pettigrew-Trimble Charge," *Gettysburg Magazine*, Volume 15, pp. 78–90. Marshall was also related to Thomas Jefferson and Gen. George Pickett.

[116]Cook, "Personal Reminiscences of Gettysburg," from *War Talks in Kansas*, p. 326.

[117]Captain J. Frank Sterling letter, July 2, 1863, 121st Pennsylvania Vertical File, GNMP.

[118]Samuel P. Bates, *The Battle of Gettysburg*, p. 66.

[119]Gates, *The Ulster Guard [20th N.Y. State Militia] and the War of the Rebellion*, p. 433; Andrew B. Cross, *The War and the Christian Commission*, p. 27.

[120]Gates, *The Ulster Guard [20th N.Y. State Militia] and the War of the Rebellion*, p. 434.

[121]Andrew B. Cross, *The War and the Christian Commission*, p. 27. This account is unique because it was written before 1865. How Capt. Little knew of the McLean family is a mystery. Perhaps he traveled to Gettysburg and was told that the property had originally belonged to Reverend McLean.

[122]*Compiler*, July 3, 1915.

[123]*Adams Sentinel*, December 8, 1863.

[124]The only Louisiana troops involved in the fighting on July 1 belonged to the brigade of Harry T. Hays, part of Jubal Early's division of Ewell's corps. They fought north of Gettysburg some distance from the Harmon farm and therefore could not have been the rebels mentioned by Amelia Harmon in her account.

[125]This theory was put forward by author and historian Scott Hartwig.

[126]*Compiler*, March 6, 1900. Lydia Meals also remembered seeing flames from the Harmon farm: "...our attention was taken up by the sight of a fire in the direction of our home. When mother [Nancy Meals] said "Lydia, I believe that is our place, and we will have to see. I said "among the Rebels," not knowing that we were surrounded by them. Some one back of me said, "where do you live miss?" I told him. "No, it is not your home, it is further away (as I found out afterward it was a house that was fired by the Confederates to oust some union

Sharpshooters)...." See ACHS Civilian Accounts.

[127]S.G. Elliot's burial map, GNMP Library.

[128]*New-York Herald*, July 3, 1863.

[129]The Herbst house was spared because there were wounded soldiers inside, one of whom was a Confederate (likely from Archer's Brigade). See the John Herbst Claims File, GNMP.

[130]John B. Bachelder, *Gettysburg: What to See, and How to See it*, p. 67; Edward Everett, *An Oration Delivered on the Battlefield of Gettysburg (November 19, 1863,) at the Consecration of the Cemetery*, p. 13; Andrew B. Cross, *Battle of Gettysburg and the Christian Commission*, p. 10.

[131]Andrew B. Cross, *The War and the Christian Commission*, p. 27.

[132]Clark, *Histories of the Several Regiments*, Volume 3, pp. 236–237.

[133]John Bachelder Maps, ACHS.

[134]OR Part 2, pp. 646-647; John B. Lindsley, *The Military Annals of Tennessee*, p. 246, 7th Tennessee Vertical File, GNMP.

[135]Bachelder Maps, ACHS; OR Part 2, pp. 664–665.

[136]OR Part 2, pp. 664–665.

[137]Ibid.

[138]Account of John L. Beveridge in *Illinois Monuments at Gettysburg*, p. 21.

[139]Marcellus Jones Journal, 8th Illinois Vertical File, GNMP.

[140]OR Part 2, pp. 664–665.

[141]Although there are conflicting accounts as to the alignment of Perrin's brigade, some of the most respected July 1 historians agree on this scenario.

[142]John A. Chapman, *History of Edgefield County, From the Earliest Settlements to 1897*, p. 487.

[143]Ibid.

[144]James F. J. Caldwell, *The History of a Brigade of South Carolinians*, p. 97.

[145]Berry Benson, *Berry Benson's Civil War Book, Memoirs of a Confederate Scout and Sharpshooter*, pp. 45–46, First South Carolina Provisional Army Vertical File, GNMP.

[146]U.R. Brooks, *Stories of the Confederacy*, pp. 37–38.

[147]*Compiler*, July 3, 1915.

[148]Varina D. Brown, *A Colonel at Gettysburg and Spotsylvania*, p. 79.

[149]J. A. Leach to John B. Bachelder, June 2, 1864, 1st South Carolina Provisional Army Vertical File, GNMP.

[150]OR Part 2, pp. 660–662.

[151]John Bachelder Maps, ACHS.

[152]OR Part 2, pp. 669–671.

[153]Fred A. Olds, "Brave Carolinian Who Fell at Gettysburg," *Southern Historical Society Papers*, Volume 36, pp. 245–247.

[154]Ibid.

[155]Ibid.

[156]Charles D. Walker, *Memorial, Virginia Military Institute*, p. 86.

[157]*Compiler*, July 3, 1915.

[158]Harry W. Pfanz, *Gettysburg The First Day*, p. 279. Various other sources indicate that Lawley was present at this time and place.

[159]OR Part 2, pp. 646–647.

[160]Clark, *Histories of Several Regiments*, Volume 3, p. 299.

[161]John D. Vautier, *History of the 88th Pennsylvania Volunteers*, p. 221. Rufus P. Northrop of the 90th Pennsylvania was likely among this group of captured Union soldiers. Based on the following account, it seems that some of these men were encamped near the John Herbst Farm. Northop wrote: "They marched us over back of Seminary Ridge, and rounded us up in a field thru which a sluggish stream ran, Marsh Creek, I think. [Northrop may be referring to Willoughby's Run instead.] We were packed together a la Andersonville, and most of us were without rations. The water in the stream was muddy and bore marks of the fighting farther up. [This is further evidence that Northrop was on the Herbst Farm, probably near Old Mill Road.] The field was off the main road a short distance up a [lane], which led to a low one-story unpainted house, where there was a spring. [This cannot be the Harmon house, as it was burned earlier that day. However, there was a spring near the Herbst house during the battle. It is still visible today.] ...The wounded men were quartered on the opposite side of the lane, and were allowed to go after water without a guard. [An 1863 Christian Commission map indicates that there was a field hospital directly across from the Herbst house along Old Mill Road.] ...I took our canteens, and watched the guard turn his back, when I slipped over among the wounded and limped down to the spring. The front yard was littered with bandages from bedding. Evidently the Johnnies had used it temporarily to care for their wounded. [In his damage claim, John Herbst mentioned that his house was used to treat wounded, and that much of his bedding was stolen or destroyed. This is further evidence that Northrop's account is of the Herbst Farm.] ...the spring was nearly dry, but I filled my canteens with an old broken spoon, and had just got them filled when a rebel Sergeant bore down on me... he took a long pull, and escorted me back without a word." This account was published in the *National Tribune* on March 23, 1911. It was given to the author by Timothy H. Smith.

[162]John B. Bachelder, *Bachelder's Illustrated Tourists Guide*, p. 26.

[163]"Gettysburg Katalysine Water," 1893 Pamphlet, Adams County Historical Society, Springs Hotel Vertical File. This vastly useful file includes many other Springs-related items that have been preserved by the society.

[164]John Bachelder Maps, ACHS.

[165]Andrew B. Cross, *The War: Battle of Gettysburg and the Christian Commission*, p. 26.

[166]John Bachelder Maps, ACHS.

[167]*Compiler*, July 3, 1915.

[168]See Kathy Georg Harrison's *Nothing But Glory, Pickett's Division at Gettysburg*, pp. 13–14.

[169]*Compiler*, July 3, 1915.

[170]Ibid.

[171]*Adams Sentinel*, July 14, 1863.

[172]See John Bachelder's Isometric Map and S. G. Elliot's Burial Map. Both maps are available online at the Library of Congress and can be downloaded in high resolution. Copies are also present at the Adams County Historical Society and at the Gettysburg National Military Park Library.

[173]Damage Claim of David Finefrock, GNMP Library (a transcribed version of the claim can be found in the Harmon Farm vertical file).

[174]*Adams Sentinel*, December 8, 1863.

[175]*Adams Sentinel*, November 21, 1865.

[176]John B. Bachelder, *Bachelder's Illustrated Tourists Guide*, p. 67.

[177]*Compiler*, March 6, 1900.

[178]Elliot Burial Map, GNMP.

[179]Dr. J. W. C. O'Neal's Medical Notebooks, ACHS; Gregory A. Coco, *Gettysburg's Confederate Dead*; Krick and Ferguson, *The Gettysburg Death Roster*.

[180]Charles D. Walker, *Memorial, Virginia Military Institute*, pp. 437–438.

[181]Dr. J.W. C. O'Neal's Medical Notebooks, ACHS; Gregory A. Coco, *Gettysburg's Confederate Dead*; Krick and Ferguson, *The Gettysburg Death Roster*.

[182]Dr. J.W.C. O'Neal Burial Journal, GNMP Library.

[183]Ibid.

[184]*Star and Sentinel*, October 5, 1877.

[185]*Compiler*, November 18, 1890.

[186]Adams County Deed Book W, p. 308.

[187]Historians Kathleen Georg Harrison and Timothy H. Smith are two exceptions, as they have correctly identified the 1863 ownership of the farm through their research.

[188]1870 United States Federal Census, Cumberland Township, Adams County, Pennsylvania; grave of David W. Finefrock, Evergreen Cemetery, Gettysburg, Pennsylvania.

[189]1880 United States Federal Census, Wilmington, New Castle, Delaware; 1900

United States Federal Census, Baltimore, Maryland; 1910 United States Federal Census, Asbury Park Ward 2, Monmouth, New Jersey. See Appendix 3.

[190]*Adams Sentinel*, November 21, 1865.

[191]Ibid.

[192]Ibid.

[193]Ibid.

[194]*Compiler*, December 18, 1865.

[195]*Compiler*, December 25, 1865; *Compiler*, November 27, 1865.

[196]*Daily National Republican*, January 6, 1866.

[197]*Compiler*, January 22, 1866.

[198]*Adams Sentinel*, April 24, 1866.

[199]*Adams Sentinel*, September 4, 1866.

[200]*Adams Sentinel*, January 1, 1867.

[201]*The Medical and Surgical Reporter*, September 28, 1867.

[202]*Star and Sentinel*, October 30, 1867.

[203]*Compiler*, November 15, 1867.

[204]Ibid.

[205]This photograph belongs to author and historian William A. Frassanito.

[206]*Compiler*, February 14, 1868.

[207]One historian wrote: "If my recollection of etymology serves me correctly, it is [a] combination of two Greek words meaning a downward flowing." This was found in the Springs Hotel Vertical File, ACHS.

[208]These distinct features were used to ward off counterfeiters.

[209]*Star and Sentinel*, January 8, 1868.

[210]*Star and Sentinel*, April 1, 1868.

[211]*Compiler*, June 26, 1868; *Star and Sentinel*, June 3, 1868.

[212]Ibid.

[213]*Star and Sentinel*, June 10, 1868.

[214]Ibid.

[215]*Star and Sentinel*, September 18, 1868. Burns himself used the Katalysine water on several occasions. See Timothy H. Smith, *John Burns, the Hero of Gettysburg*, p. 122.

[216]*Compiler*, August 28, 1868.

[217]*Star and Sentinel*, September 11, 1868.

[218]*Star and Sentinel*, October 16, 1868.

[219]*Compiler*, November 20, 1868.

[220]Ibid.; *Star and Sentinel*, December 4, 1868; *Star and Sentinel*, October 30, 1868.

[221]*Star and Sentinel*, October 30, 1868.

[222]*Star and Sentinel*, March 19, 1869.

[223]*Star and Sentinel*, February 19, 1869.

[224]*Star and Sentinel*, April 2, 1869; 1870 United States Federal Census, Cumberland Township, Adams County, Pennsylvania.

[225]*New York Times*, April 3, 1869.

[226]Ibid.

[227]*Daily Evening Bulletin*, April 10, 1869. A similar article appeared in the *New York Times*.

[228]It is unclear where Emanuel Harmon lived during the late 1860s and early 1870s. He appears on the 1870 Septennial Census in Cumberland Township but apparently moved to New York City in about 1873. His 1876 death certificate stated that he was a resident of New York City at the time of his death.

[229]*Compiler*, April 9, 1869; *Compiler*, April 23, 1869.

[230]*Star and Sentinel*, May 16, 1869.

[231]Ibid.; *New York Times*, June 1, 1869; *Star and Sentinel*, June 25, 1869.

[232]*Compiler*, July 2, 1869; *Star and Sentinel*, July 9, 1869.

[233]*Star and Sentinel*, July 9, 1869.

[234]*Compiler*, July 2, 1869; *Compiler*, July 16, 1869; *Star and Sentinel*, July 16, 1869; *Star and Sentinel*, July 23, 1869. The location of these bathhouses may have been between the Mill Road and the hotel.

[235]*Daily Evening Bulletin*, August 5, 1869; *Star and Sentinel*, August 6, 1869; *Star and Sentinel*, August 27, 1869.

[236]*Compiler*, August 20, 1869; *Star and Sentinel*, September 2, 1869.

[237]*Compiler*, September 24, 1869; *Star and Sentinel*, June 17, 1870. The location of the billiard/bowling house is not known. It may have been located behind the hotel near the stable. The ice house was constructed east of Willoughby's Run on the edge of the lake.

[238]*New York Times*, June 16, 1870; *Star and Sentinel*, July 1, 1870; *Star and Sentinel*, July 15, 1870. Maybe the water killed him.

[239]1870 United States Federal Census, Cumberland Township, Adams County, Pennsylvania.

[240]*Star and Sentinel*, August 26, 1870.

[241]*Compiler*, June 9, 1871; *Compiler*, June 30, 1871.

[242]"Out of the Past," *Gettysburg Times*, August 23, 1971; Author's collection; *New York Tribune*, April 4, 1872; *Sacramento Daily Union*, June 5, 1872.

[243]*Compiler*, May 31, 1872.

[244]John B. Bachelder, *Bachelder's Illustrated Tourists Guide*, pp. 108–109.

[245]*Star and Sentinel*, August 12, 1875. The quarry is located just east of Willoughby's Run on the edge of the McPherson farm. A path behind the 7th Wisconsin monument leads to this location.

[246]*Compiler*, March 2, 1876. An index to Brooklyn death records indicates that Harmon was 58 years old at the time of his death.

[247]J. W. C. O'Neal, *Contribution to the History and Use of the Katalysine Spring Water, at Gettysburg.*

[248]*Compiler*, July 26, 1877.

[249]*Star and Sentinel*, May 17, 1878. This article was brought to the author's attention by historian Timothy H. Smith.

[250]*Compiler*, July 17, 1879.

[251]*Daily National Republican*, July 8, 1881.

[252]*Richmond Dispatch*, July 8, 1886.

[253]*St. Paul Daily Globe*, July 10, 1886.

[254]*Compiler*, May 10, 1887. Henry Yingling was also involved in operating the Eagle Hotel in Gettysburg at this time.

[255]*Compiler*, July 12, 1887.

[256]*National Tribune*, June 12, 1888.

[257]*National Tribune*, July 12, 1888.

[258]*Pittsburg Dispatch*, September 7, 1889.

[259]Gettysburg Springs Hotel pamphlet, 1894, Springs Hotel Vertical File, ACHS.

[260]Account of Flo Blocher Arnold, 1956, Springs Hotel Vertical File, ACHS.

[261]William G. Weaver, "Reminiscences of Gettysburg," April 21, 1969, Springs Hotel Vertical File, ACHS.

[262]Ibid.

[263]*Gettysburg Times*, August 16, 1909.

[264]*Gettysburg Times*, May 13, 1913. This article was merely an attempt to convince the public that the spring's popularity was as great as it had once been.

[265]*Gettysburg Times*, June 16, 1913.

[266]*Gettysburg Times*, May 13, 1914; *Gettysburg Times*, March 8, 1916; *Gettysburg Times*, June 13, 1917.

[267]*Gettysburg Times*, December 17, 1917. According to this article, the fire originated "from a flue in the wall between the second and third floor."

[268]Ibid.

[269]*Gettysburg Times*, February 13, 1920; *Gettysburg Times*, June 29, 1920.

[270]*Compiler*, May 11, 1935.

[271]Ibid.

[272]*Gettysburg Times*, June 15, 1935.

[273]*Gettysburg Times*, August 2, 1935; *Gettysburg Times*, August 20, 1935; *Gettysburg Times*, September 1, 1935.

[274]*Gettysburg Times*, July 21, 1947.

[275]Ibid.

[276]Ibid.

[277]Ibid.

[278]Ibid.; "History of the Gettysburg Country Club, 1948–1998," unpublished manuscript, Gettysburg Country Club Vertical File, ACHS.

[279]"History of the Gettysburg Country Club, 1948–1998," unpublished manuscript, Gettysburg Country Club Vertical File, ACHS.

[280]Ibid.

[281]Ibid. This building was demolished in recent years to make room for new tennis courts.

[282]*Gettysburg Times*, July 13, 1948.

[283]"History of the Gettysburg Country Club, 1948–1998," unpublished manuscript, Gettysburg Country Club Vertical File, ACHS. These trails are visible on a 1957 aerial photograph of the Gettysburg area. This and other early aerial photographs can be viewed at http://www.pennpilot.psu.edu. A 1937 aerial photograph of the property clearly shows debris from the Springs Hotel.

[284]This building no longer stands, nor does the golf-cart barn. The latter structure was recently demolished by the National Park Service in order to restore the land to its 1863 appearance.

[285]*Gettysburg Times*, April 4, 1955.

[286]*Stars and Stripes*, May 28, 1956.

[287]*Stars and Stripes*, June 23, 1957.

[288]*Stars and Stripes*, June 23, 1957.

[289]U. S. Department of the Interior News Release, March 25, 2011; *Gettysburg Times*, March 26, 2011.

[290]William A. Frassanito, *Early Photography at Gettysburg*, pp. 35–36, 40.

[291]*Star and Sentinel*, November 13, 1868.

Bibliography

Newspapers

Adams Sentinel, Gettysburg, Pennsylvania

Charlotte Daily Observer, Charlotte, North Carolina

Daily Evening Bulletin, Philadelphia, Pennsylvania

Daily National Republican, Washington, D.C.

Gettysburg Compiler, Gettysburg, Pennsylvania

Gettysburg Times, Gettysburg, Pennsylvania

National Tribune, Washington, D.C.

New York Herald, New York, New York

New York Times, New York, New York

New-York Tribune, New York, New York

Pittsburg Dispatch, Pittsburgh, Pennsylvania

Richmond Dispatch, Richmond, Virginia

Sacramento Daily Union, Sacramento, California

St. Paul Daily Globe, St. Paul, Minnesota

Star and Sentinel, Gettysburg, Pennsylvania

Stars and Stripes, Honolulu, Hawaii

Manuscripts

Adams County Historical Society, Gettysburg, PA:
  1858 Adams County Converse Map
  1872 Adams County Atlas
  Adams County Deed Books
  Adams County Tax Records
  Donald R. Heiges, "The Gettysburg Springs Hotel"
  Estate Files
  Gettysburg Country Club Vertical File
  J.W.C. O'Neal Papers
  Jacob M. Sheads, *The Burning of the Home of General 'Stonewall' Jackson's Uncle by the Rebels during the First Day's Battle of Gettysburg, July 1, 1863*
  John B. Bachelder Maps
  Springs Hotel Vertical File
  United States Census Records
  W.C. Storrick Papers

Gettysburg National Military Park, Gettysburg, Pennsylvania:
  Battlefield Farm Files

Civilian Damage Claim Files
Kathleen Georg Harrison, "The Significance of the Harmon Farm and the Springs Hotel Woods"
News Releases
Regimental Vertical Files
S.G. Elliot Burial Map

National Archives and Research Administration, Washington, D.C.:
Pension and Service Records

York County Historical Society, York, Pennsylvania:
Estate Files

Books/Articles

Bachelder, John B. *Bachelder's Illustrated Tourist's Guide of the United States. Popular Resorts, and How to Reach Them*. Boston, MA: John B. Bachelder, 1873.

Bachelder, John B. *Gettysburg: What to See and How to See it*. Boston, MA: John B. Bachelder, 1878.

Bates, Samuel P. *The Battle of Gettysburg*. Philadelphia, PA: T.H. Davis & Co., 1875.

Beecham, Robert K. Gettysburg, *The Pivotal Battle of the Civil War*. Chicago, IL: A.C. McClurg & Co., 1911.

Bell, John. "On the Medical Properties of the Gettysburg Mineral Spring." *The Medical and Surgical Reporter*, vol. 17.

Beveridge, John L., and others, *Illinois Monuments at Gettysburg*. Springfield, IL: H.W. Rokker, 1892.

Biographical Directory of the United States Congress 1774–2005. Washington, DC: U.S. Government Printing Office, 2005.

Bradford, Thomas L. *Biographical Index of the Graduates of the Homeopathic Medical College of Pennsylvania and the Hahnemann Medical College and Hospital of Philadelphia*. Lancaster, PA: Achey & Gorrecht, 1918.

Brown, Varina D. *A Colonel at Gettysburg and Spotsylvania*. Columbia, SC: The State Company, 1931.

Caldwell, J.F.J. *The History of a Brigade of South Carolinians First Known as "Gregg's" and Subsequently as "McGowan's"*. Philadelphia, PA: King & Baird, 1866.

Calef, John H. "Gettysburg Notes: The Opening Gun." *Journal of the Military Service Institution of the United States*, vol. 40 (1907): 40–58.

Chapman, John A. *History of Edgefield County, From the Earliest Settlements to 1897*. Newberry, SC: Elbert H. Aull, 1897.

Clark, Walter. *Histories of the Several Regiments and Battalions from North Carolina in the Great War 1861–'65*. 3 vols. Goldsboro, NC: Nash Brothers, 1901.

Coco, Gregory A. *Gettysburg's Confederate Dead.* Gettysburg, PA: Thomas Publications, 2003.

Cole, J. Timothy and Bradley R. Foley. *Collett Leventhorpe, the English Confederate, the life of a Civil War General, 1815–1889.* Jefferson, NC: McFarland & Company, inc., 2007.

Confederate Veteran Magazine. 40 vols. (1893-1932).

Cook, John D.S. "Personal Reminiscences of Gettysburg." *War Talks in Kansas.* Kansas City, MO: Franklin Hudson Publishing Company, 1906.

Cross, Andrew B. *The War. Battle of Gettysburg and the Christian Commission.* Baltimore, MD: 1865.

Curtis, Orson B. *History of the Twenty-Fourth Michigan of the Iron Brigade Known as the Detroit and Wayne County Regiment.* Detroit, MI: Winn & Hammond, 1891.

Davis, Archie K. *Boy Colonel of the Confederacy: The Life and Times of Henry King Burgwyn, Jr.* Chapel Hill, NC: University of North Carolina Press, 1985.

Everett, Edward. *An Oration Delivered on the Battlefield of Gettysburg (November 19, 1863,) at the Consecration of the Cemetery.* New York, NY: Baker & Godwin, 1863.

Frassanito, William A. *Early Photography at Gettysburg.* Gettysburg, PA: Thomas Publications, 1995.

Gaff, Alan D. "'Here Was Made Our Last and Hopeless Stand' The 'Lost' Gettysburg Reports of the Nineteenth Indiana" *Gettysburg Magazine.* vol. 2.

Gates, Theodore B. *The "Ulster Guard" [20th N.Y. State Militia] and the War of the Rebellion.* New York, NY: Benjamin H. Tyrrel, 1879.

Harrison, Kathy Georg. *Nothing But Glory, Pickett's Division at Gettysburg.* Gettysburg, PA: Thomas Publications, 1987.

History of the 121st Regiment Pennsylvania Volunteers. Revised Edition. Philadelphia, PA: Press of Catholic Standard and Times, 1906.

Junkin, D.X. *The Reverend George Junkin, D.D., LL.D. A History and Biography.* Philadelphia, PA: J.B. Lippincott & Co., 1871.

Krick, Robert K., and Chris L. Ferguson. *The Gettysburg Death Roster, the Confederate Dead at Gettysburg,* Fourth Edition, Revised. Dayton, OH: Morningside Bookshop/Press, 2004.

Ladd, David L., and Audrey J. Ladd, eds. *The Bachelder Papers.* Dayton, OH: Morningside House, 1994.

New York Monuments Commission for the Battlefields of Gettysburg and Chattanooga. Final Report on the Battlefield of Gettysburg. 3 vols. Albany, NY: J.B. Lyon Company, 1900.

O'Neal, J. W.C. *Contribution to the History and Use of the Katalysine Spring Water, at Gettysburg.* Gettysburg, PA: H.J. Stahle, 1876.

Osborne, Seward R. *Holding the Left at Gettysburg: The 20th New York State Militia on July 1, 1863*. Hightstown, NJ: Longstreet House, 1990.

Pennsylvania at Gettysburg, Ceremonies at the Dedication of the Monuments Erected by the Commonwealth of Pennsylvania. 2 vols. Harrisburg, PA: E.K. Meyers, 1893.

Pfanz, Harry W. *Gettysburg, the First Day*. Chapel Hill, NC: University of North Carolina Press, 2001.

Smith, Timothy H. *John Burns, the Hero of Gettysburg*. Gettysburg, PA: Thomas Publications, 2000.

Southern Historical Society Papers. 52 vols. (1876-1927).

Stine, James H. *History of the Army of the Potomac*. Washington, DC: Gibson Brothers, 1893.

Taylor, Michael W. "Col. James Keith Marshall: One of Three Brigade Commanders Killed in the Pickett-Pettigrew-Trimble Charge." *Gettysburg Magazine*, vol. 15.

The War of the Rebellion: A Compilation of the Official Records of the Union and Confederate Armies. 128 vols. in 4 series. Washington, D.C.; U.S. Government Printing Office, 1880-1901.

The Water Cure Journal, vol. 13 and 18. New York, NY: 1852, 1854.

U.R. Brooks, ed. *Stores of the Confederacy*. Columbia, SC: The State Company, 1912.

Vail, Enos B. *Reminiscences of a Boy in the Civil War*. Brooklyn, NY: Enos B. Vail, 1915.

Vautier, John D. *History of the Eighty-Eighth Pennsylvania Volunteers in the War for the Union, 1861-1865*. Philadelphia, PA: J.B. Lippincott & Co., 1894.

Walker, Charles D. *Memorial, Virginia Military Institute*. Biographical Sketches of the Graduates and Eleves of the Virginia Military Institute Who Fell During the War Between the States. Philadelphia, PA: J.B. Lippincott & Co., 1875.

Websites

www.ancestry.com

www.familysearch.com

www.findagrave.com

www.fold3.com

www.google.com/patents

www.pennpilot.psu.edu

Index

About the Author

Andrew I. Dalton is a volunteer at the Gettysburg National Military Park and the Adams County Historical Society. He lives in Gettysburg, Pennsylvania, near the Harmon farm and is currently a sophomore at Gettysburg Area High School. In recent years he has given lectures and walking tours of the Harmon farm for local historical groups.